THE HISTORY OF GUNSTOCK

THE HISTORY OF GUNSTOCK

SKIING IN THE BELKNAP MOUNTAINS

CAROL LEE ANDERSON

FOREWORD BY PENNY PITOU

THE History PRESS

Published by The History Press
Charleston, SC 29403
www.historypress.net

Front cover illustration by Carol Lee Anderson. Back cover photos courtesy of the Gunstock Area Commission

First published 2011
Second printing 2013

Manufactured in the United States

ISBN 978.1.60949.136.9

Anderson, Carol Lee, 1962-
The history of Gunstock : skiing in the Belknap mountains / Carol Lee Anderson.
p. cm.
Includes bibliographical references and index.
ISBN 978-1-60949-136-9
1. Skis and skiing--New Hampshire--Belknap County--History. 2. Ski resorts--New Hampshire--Belknap County--History. I. Title.
GV854.5.N4A64 2011
796.9309742'45--dc23
2011033915

This book is dedicated to Torger Tokle, whose amazing life and heroic death will forever remain an inspiration to me.

Sempre Avanti

A plaque honoring Torger Tokle stands stoically at the base of Gunstock's Torger Tokle Memorial Ski Jump. *Photo by Harrison Haas.*

CONTENTS

Contents

FOREWORD

Growing up in Gilford gave me a perspective on life that I doubt I could have ever received anywhere else. To live right next door to such a gifted man as Gary Allen and to have access to his talent and patience—as well as his barn full of used skis—allowed my life, goals and ambitions to blossom in a most unique and special way.

My childhood was fostered by my wonderful parents and was filled with careful guidance, but at the same time, it was a carefree existence. We were allowed time to relax, lie in the grass, look up at the sky and dream our dreams. That amazing feeling I had as a child is carried with me always and is the same feeling I get when I put on a pair of skis and fly down a mountain, whether here in the States or somewhere in the Alps.

I get homesick very easily, and even though there is an entire world of places in which I could have chosen to live, I just couldn't have lived anywhere except right here in my hometown of Gilford. It has kept me young to look out to the field where I used to play as a child—that same field is now my front yard. Just up the road are the slopes on which we learned to ski as young, energetic members of the Gilford Outing Club.

The Gilford Outing Club was an organization beyond compare. Never have I seen a volunteer group produce so many fine young people who have become the best at what they do. We have often tried to figure out what was so special about the Gilford Outing Club, but I honestly believe that it was a combination of the patience, talent, hard work and love for the next generation that made it one of a kind. The parents who volunteered week after week throughout the entire year left all of us with attitudes toward life that made us feel that anything was possible and that there was nothing to stop us from attaining our goals, no matter how lofty.

Later on, when I needed more of a challenge, the adventures I had at Gunstock only added to my pleasant memories. As a child, I can remember riding that amazing single chairlift up Mount Rowe and skiing down the backside of the mountain to my home. By today's standards that lift now seems archaic, especially since its chairs would sometimes skim the ground at the high spots. But oh, how great it was to ride up the mountain!

I took my first and only ski lesson with Maynard Libby at the Area and soared from the ten- and twenty-meter jumps after school on bitterly cold evenings. Endless hours were spent skiing with friends there, training and racing on Fletcher Hale. In 1961, my husband, Egon Zimmermann, and I took over the ski school, and our two sons, Christian and Kim, learned to ski there. My grandchildren, Dylan, Zane and Zoe, now ride the lifts and schuss down the new trails at Gunstock.

My life story has become part of the history of this ski area. We all hope that our lives and accomplishments will take on their own meaning and provide inspiration to future generations. In order for that to happen, though, they must be set on paper. The writing and publication of this book is the perfect way to accomplish that goal.

I first met Carol Anderson when she was working with her daughter on the restoration of the warm-up hut used by the Gilford Outing Club. That building means so much to me, and I was very pleased to see someone working to preserve it. Over time, I watched her dedication toward this history grow, and her commitment to its preservation is unrivaled.

I told her when she became the first president of the Gunstock Mountain Historic Preservation Society that only she could hold that position. I believe that only she could write this book. We have discussed this history over a number of years, and she has been a pit bull when it comes to the research, never leaving a stone unturned until every avenue has been exhausted. The task has been a daunting one, but the respect she has for the individuals who make up the story of Gunstock is immense, and it shows.

Foreword

This is a book that needed to be written, and it brings us all a certain sense of relief that this information is here now in one place, for us, our children and our grandchildren. It is a gift for all to enjoy.

Penny Pitou
Gilford, New Hampshire
February 2011

ACKNOWLEDGEMENTS

I offer my sincerest gratitude to Penny Pitou, who has spent countless hours telling me her stories and explaining the history of skiing in the Lakes Region. I was deeply honored, and still am, when she agreed to write the foreword for this book. Her great affection for Gilford's history is apparent in the tremendous support she shows, in so many different ways, for its preservation. She is a wonderful, caring friend and completely understands the magic I see in our ski history.

My appreciation goes out to the Gunstock Area Commission and to the management and staff of Gunstock Mountain Resort, especially Doug Irving and Chelsea Smith, for their patience and professionalism when answering my never-ending questions.

Greg Goddard, general manager of Gunstock, has been supportive of my efforts to preserve the history of the ski area he manages from the first moment I contacted him. He responds to my many requests immediately and is always there to smooth my path, and his generosity has been a tremendous help to me. His input, guidance and hard work as an officer and director of the Gunstock Mountain Historic Preservation Society have been priceless.

Bill Quigley, director of sales and marketing at Gunstock, dug around in the attic of the Main Lodge, discovered Gunstock's historic documents and brought them to everyone's attention. He is always such a great help, and I am so thankful that his actions preserved such an important history. His idea of a book about Gunstock arrived just at the right time in my life.

I am forever indebted to Bob Durfee of the Gunstock Area Commission, who spent countless hours flattening, organizing and cataloguing the historic blueprints at Gunstock. He spent just as many hours trying to find answers to my long list of questions. He also selflessly lent his time, energy and organizational skills to the Gunstock Mountain Historic Preservation Society during its formation and beyond. Bob's dedication to the ski area, its history and prosperity is second to none.

Diane Mitton, curator for Gilford's Thompson-Ames Historical Society, answered the call of duty when Bill Quigley asked her to stop by and assess Gunstock's historic documents. She spent hours upon hours up in the lodge attic organizing the boxes of photos. Her work with those photos helped me visualize and understand Gunstock's history, making it far easier for me to choose some of the images for this book.

Jeff Leich, executive director of the New England Ski Museum, met with me well before I began to write this book. His ideas and suggestions made it much quicker for me to form the outline of this book. I also thank Linda Bradshaw of the ski museum for providing quick answers to my last-minute questions, as well as for her enthusiasm.

The librarians and staff of the Laconia Public Library cheerfully came to my aid when I needed it as I sat in front of the microfilm machine for what seemed an eternity. They never once complained as they replaced the ink cartridges I helped empty as I made more than eight hundred copies of pertinent newspaper articles.

Gunstock Inn owners Maurine and Dick Bastille were more than happy to help me try to piece together the history of their historic inn, originally known as the Baraks. They are both historians at heart, and I am thankful that they understand and preserve as much of the inn's history as is humanly possible.

I completely enjoyed listening to the amazing stories of Gunstock's history told to me by John Veazey, who sadly passed away at the end of 2010. He was always willing to listen to my ideas and answer my questions, whether by phone or in person. His firsthand knowledge of this history was amazing, and I sincerely appreciate his willingness to share his memories, as well as his sense of humor. I thank him from the bottom of my heart for saving those historic blueprints that tell us the story of the development of this ski area. He is sorely missed.

With people like Bob Bolduc in the world, it is guaranteed that history will forever be preserved. He loves to surround himself with history and has one of the most extensive personal collections of historical ski artifacts of anyone I know. A great storyteller, he has given me a wealth of information and background into the people who made our ski history so special. Bob is a great friend and is always there on the other end of the phone offering information and help when I need it.

It is touching to see the care and pride with which Bob Arnold, grandson of Fritzie Baer, preserves his family's history. Because of Bob's help, through our conversations, e-mails and exchanges of documents and photos, I have been able to write with confidence about his "Grampa Baer." He has spent an enormous amount of time researching the years his grandfather was manager at the Area, and as a director of the Gunstock Mountain Historic Preservation Society, he is always willing to lend a helping hand.

Bernie Dion Sr., a member of the Amazing Jumping Dions, has never failed to keep me laughing with his stories of the years when he was an Olympic-level ski jumper, as well as those when he was an FIS official and a coach to all the "little munchkins." Now, as a director of the preservation society at Gunstock, he freely lends his expertise in many different ways. I find his great outlook on life endlessly enjoyable.

Sara Allen, wife of the late Gary Allen, was incredibly helpful to me while I was writing this book and in other aspects of my life as well. I could never have kept track of Gary's accomplishments without her guidance. She is an amazing and inspirational woman not only to me but also to so many others in the community.

Brian Trudgeon and Alison Thibodeau, children of Bill Trudgeon, have been so supportive of my efforts and always quickly answer the questions I have about the time when their father became part of the fabric of Gunstock's history. They are both wonderful people, and in them I can see the greatness of their father.

I thank Ruth McLaughlin, president of the Gunstock Ski Club, for replying to my endless e-mails and for supplying me with a wealth of information about the history of her club. She read the words "Just one more question" far too many times!

It has been exciting getting to know Peter Hussey, son of Philip W. Hussey Sr. He never hesitated to help me gain more information about the important work that his father did while in Gilford. The Hussey family, as well as the employees of the Hussey Seating Company, couldn't be a more pleasant and helpful group of people. It is no surprise to me this company has been successfully run for 176 years.

Writer, journalist and photographer Scott Andrews is also a dedicated director and curator for the Ski Museum of Maine. He has been one of the biggest supporters of the jump project at Gunstock and has been one of my most enthusiastic cheerleaders, for which I can never thank him enough.

Preservation consultant Elizabeth Durfee Hengen and historian Sarah Delangelas Hofe were both working to create a superb Historic Resources Study on Gunstock Mountain Resort at the same time I was writing this book. I so enjoyed our lively exchanges of photos and information. Our love of history created a bond between us that got us through the sometimes daunting task of researching the history of this ski area.

I am in awe of the artistic talents of photographers such as Harold J. Piper, Loran Percy and Dave Buckman, who have captured so many beautiful images of Gunstock, all of which have now become part of its permanent archives. Many appear in this book. I thank the Gunstock Area Commission for granting me permission to use the images.

Some of the most amazing photographs ever taken of Gunstock are part of the personal collection of Raymond Reed. His willingness to share them with me is greatly appreciated, and I will always be grateful to him for allowing me to use them in this book.

It meant the world to me when I asked Kenneth Tokle for photographs of his late uncle, Torger Tokle, and he immediately produced the most amazing group of pictures depicting the special energy Torger possessed. I am thrilled to be able to include some of those images in this book. Ken and his wife, Nina, are two incredibly special people.

We should all thank Earl Norem for his service to this country when he served as a member of the Tenth Mountain Division during World War II. I thank him for his openness when sharing his heartbreaking story of carrying the body of Torger Tokle down from the mountains in Italy. He has courageously carried that memory with him for an entire lifetime.

Bill Duncan was a personal friend of Torger Tokle, and as a member of the Tenth Mountain Division, he was just a few yards away when Torger was killed during World War II. His philosophy on the tough training at Camp Hale and what he witnessed during the war is truly inspiring and could only come from one belonging to the Greatest Generation. I have the utmost respect for him and all of the members of the Tenth Mountain Division.

To all at The History Press, especially commissioning editor Jeff Saraceno and project editor Ryan Finn, I cannot ever thank you properly for all of the help and hard work that went into the publication of this book and for believing in my writing. It has been a wonderful experience working with such encouraging and professional people.

I first met Harrison Haas during an interview for an article he was writing as a reporter for the *Citizen of Laconia*, and since then, he has become like a son to me and a treasured friend to my family. It was a delight to watch how effortlessly he captured the essence of this history in the contemporary images that appear in this book. He has the ability to see the extraordinary in the ordinary, and I am proud to be able to showcase his photography within these pages.

Lastly, I am eternally grateful to my husband, John, and our two children, Sarah and Dean, for never failing to support my highly ambitious goals and for taking the time to stop and smell the roses with me. Only they know how much of my life went into the writing of this book, and they were there to help me every step of the way. Our family life is, and always will be, the ultimate gift.

INTRODUCTION

The devastating effects of the Great Depression brought financial disaster to the Lakes Region of central New Hampshire, as it did to the rest of America. The small, sleepy town of Gilford, located on the picturesque shores of Lake Winnipesaukee, saw its fair share of hardship and heartache during this difficult era. Nevertheless, it was a community occupied by individuals who were dedicated to helping one another through the hard times.

This dedication set the stage for the development of the Belknap Mountains Recreation Area during the 1930s, an outstanding example of the American work ethic and what can be accomplished when it is used to its fullest. The stories behind this project show how these talented individuals solved difficult problems, overcame seemingly insurmountable obstacles and, in so many cases, used incredible ingenuity to make something from nothing. Most times, it seemed as if nothing came easy for these people. Their stories take us on a continual roller coaster ride. Yet each story leaves behind a tale of a commitment to nothing but excellence.

The history of today's Gunstock Mountain Resort (formerly the Belknap Mountains Recreation Area) is filled with the names of organizations and individuals who have accomplished great feats, from the Hussey Manufacturing Company, builder of the ski area, to Penny Pitou, winner of two Silver Medals at the 1960 Winter Olympics. Entwined in the stories of the well-known personalities of Gunstock are the life stories of unsung heroes in the community. Sadly, many of these names have already been forgotten.

A chapter is dedicated to Torger Tokle, the Norwegian ski jumping sensation who became a household name during the late 1930s. Known to those who are involved in the sport today but not commonly known to the general public, his ever-optimistic view of life, his amazing accomplishments and his tragic death hold life lessons for us all.

During my initial research of the Gilford Outing Club, it became obvious that there was a certain type of magic that swirled through the community, and it continued through all of the local ski history. It was evident in the creation of the Belknap Mountains Recreation Area, it showed itself during the times when the Area was in jeopardy of being lost forever and it continues into the present-day resort. The children who were fortunate enough to grow up in this atmosphere have become leaders in their professions and communities, proof that there was definitely something astir in the nondescript, rural town of Gilford.

Because of the important lessons to be learned from all of this, it became imperative that these stories be documented; thus the idea for this book was born. It is a record of history, but it was written to honor all of those who changed the community by building and maintaining the Belknap Mountains Recreation Area throughout the years, from the skiing stars who put the ski area on the map to those who dedicated countless hours teaching and molding our future leaders through the sport of skiing.

SKIING TAKES THE LAKES REGION BY STORM

There was a certain peaceful silence back then in Gilford; the only noise you heard was the sound of the cowbells as the cows grazed across the pasture.
—Shirley Faller, member of the Phelps family of Gilford

The history of Gunstock Mountain Resort is a fascinating and unique story of the spirit of community, constant struggle and innovation, the evolution of skiing stars and resident Olympians. The all-season recreation area is located in an unlikely place: the small rural New England town of Gilford, which is nestled in the central portion of New Hampshire. From the time the town became incorporated in 1812 until the creation of the Belknap Mountains Recreation Area (today's Gunstock), Gilford existed as a peaceful farming community. Located within Belknap County, its pre-skiing landscape included a picturesque shoreline on the south side of Lake Winnipesaukee, vast open pastures and several mountains belonging to the Belknap Mountain Range.

This range, which offers breathtaking views from its summits, has been visited by thousands of people each year. Before being known as the Belknaps, the range was known as the Blue Mountains, named for the annual abundant crop of wild, low-bush blueberries. Two of the mountains in this range played an important role in the development of skiing in the Lakes Region. The first, Mount Rowe, stands modestly at 1,600 feet. The second, Gunstock Mountain, situated adjacent to Mount Rowe, appears to dwarf its neighbor with an elevation of just over 2,300 feet.

The pre-skiing landscape of Gilford included farmhouses, barns and rolling pastures, all with a backdrop of mountains. *Courtesy of Thompson-Ames Historical Society.*

Farmers who lived and worked around these mountains cleared the land for pasture, leaving only the uppermost portions of them as forest. A high percentage of the land throughout the town was maintained as open pasture; the farmers had unknowingly created the perfect landscape for skiing.

During the onset of the Great Depression, many of the area's farmers were unaffected by the financial crisis gripping the entire nation. However, as the decade began to unfold, more and more abandoned farms began to dot the landscape. As the economic difficulties continued, local residents became worried about their future, and they searched for a light at the end of the tunnel.

That bright spot had already arrived, and it was the sport of skiing. Considered only a pastime at first, it was rapidly capturing the attention and interest of local residents and visitors alike. Laconia, being surrounded by lakes, was already an established summer vacation destination. In a natural progression, the same vacationers began to return during the winter. Ice fishing, boating and sled dog racing through the main streets of Laconia were already extremely popular sports, the latter dominating the headlines during the winter months. Recreationalists also enjoyed ice skating and sledding along with auto and horse racing on the frozen lake.

The Winnipesaukee Ski Club, established in 1918, was undeniably responsible for the rapid development of skiing, first in Laconia and then in Gilford. The club was known throughout the nation for its enthusiastic promotion of the sport—it was an organization composed of highly dedicated individuals. By 1931, the club had almost one hundred sustaining members. Its focus and mission was to promote winter sports on an amateur basis, and it became a major social outlet for local residents, hosting hikes, plays, ski balls, skating races and competitive ski meets.

Upon the arrival of skiing in the Lakes Region, the Nordic discipline dominated with its exciting spectator sport of ski jumping. Smaller ski jumps were already being used by the ski club in Laconia. In the early 1920s, a fifteen-meter jump was in constant use on Mile Hill. A few years later, a twenty-meter hill was built on Mechanic Street. The ski jumps, ironically, were built next to cemeteries and in tight traffic flow areas. Local traffic often had to be stopped in order for jumpers to land safely. This disruption did not meet with any opposition from drivers, who found this new obstacle positively fascinating.

Ski jumping found its way to neighboring Gilford in 1930 with the construction of a monstrous jump and a log cabin on the Morin farm on Cotton Hill. Built by the Winnipesaukee Ski Club, the structure was 195 feet high and 236 feet long with a price tag of $2,500. The jump was used until the end of March 1932, at which time it was destroyed during a fierce wind and snowstorm. The howling wind was strong enough to rip the massive structure off its footings and send it crashing in pieces to the ground. The cost to repair the existing structure was estimated at $3,000, causing the idea of reconstructing the jump to be abandoned. Members of the club decided that a completely different location for a new jump would have to be found.[1]

Seizing the opportunity to transport winter sport enthusiasts, the Boston & Maine Railroad began to run trains, called snow trains, from Boston to the Lakes Region. One train each Sunday brought several hundred members of the Appalachian Mountain Club to Laconia, with more passengers continuing to northern ski areas. Individuals from the mountain club were entertained by the Winnipesaukee Ski Club, which provided buses to various activities such as ski jumping, skiing, snowshoe hikes, sled dog races and ice fishing.

As the Lakes Region developed into a mecca for winter sports and activities, there were many organizations and individuals in the region who were visionaries and could see the potential benefits. Besides the

Winnipesaukee Ski Club, the Laconia Chamber of Commerce, the Laconia Rotary Club, the Elks and the Kiwanis Club were all organizations supporting winter sports in the area. The local landscape had everything required: the lake, mountains and plenty of snow during the winter months. Beyond that, they also saw the potential for year-round activities, with the lake offering the perfect environment for summer sports and the mountains offering thousands of scenic acres for hiking.

Attorney Park Carpenter of Boston, head of the Appalachian Mountain Club, was one of the first individuals to promote the idea of a major ski area being located in the Lakes Region. He fell in love with skiing while studying at Dartmouth College in 1914, skied near Boston in the early 1920s and became a member of the Boston-based White Mountain Ski Runners. Members of the Winnipesaukee Ski Club who were familiar with his interest in the sport urged him to explore the terrain in the Lakes Region to see if he felt it was suitable for skiing. Many in the area felt that the elevation of the mountains in Gilford was not high enough to challenge any intermediate or advanced skier.

A meeting was arranged between members of the Winnipesaukee Ski Club and Park Carpenter. On a Sunday in February 1931, a snow train brought him to Laconia to meet with Gilford resident Gordon Langill, a highly active member of the ski club. Gordon was chosen to lead a party of more than one hundred individuals sporting snowshoes up Gunstock Mountain, down through the wooded area over to neighboring Belknap Mountain and then down again. After the long, brisk hike, the group unanimously decided that the landscape was more than suitable for the development of a ski center.

Langill worked with other club members to draw up preliminary plans for a twenty-six-mile, third-class trail system through the Belknap Mountain Range. These trails had already been informally mapped out by the club, and after final plans were approved, work began on cutting the trails that fall. Among the trail names chosen were Winnipesaukee, Belknap, Gunstock, Piper, Rowe, Stone Bar, Corkscrew and Ridge.

Volunteers from the Winnipesaukee Ski Club, Appalachian Mountain Club and White Mountain Ski Runners spent hundreds of hours cutting trees, clearing brush and removing rocks on Belknap Mountain. Dynamite was used in some cases to blast away the biggest of boulders. Members also posted triangular markers on the trails and utilized a type of sign language to let skiers know what to expect ahead on the trails.

In total, the ambitious group cut about fifteen miles of trails through some of the mountains in the range, including Rowe, Gunstock, Belknap, Cobble, Piper, Whiteface and Grant Mountains, as well as on Mount Major. These trails were known as the Belknap Range Ridge Ski Trails, or the Belknaps for short. This network of trails was the most extensive in the East, and by 1932 many had been completed. They quickly became known as the most outstanding trails in the region and consistently received high approval ratings from skiers.

It came as no surprise when the Eastern Amateur Ski Association awarded its first Eastern Downhill Championship Race to the Winnipesaukee Ski Club. It was held on the popular Belknap Ridge Trail in January 1932 and was followed shortly thereafter by the Eastern Championship Race held on February 21.

These championship races got the attention of even more influential individuals. Another steadfast fan of skiing, Captain Edward Lydiard, director of the Eastern Amateur Ski Association, did not hesitate to become deeply entwined in the development of the sport in the Lakes Region. In December 1934, he led a twenty-four-hour drive to raise $500 to build a second-class trail on Belknap Mountain and firmly believed that this type of trail would be needed to secure the reputation of the area as a ski attraction.[2] Simultaneously, a group of engineers came forward and offered to build a ski tow in the area if the second-class trail became a reality. With this offer on the table, the money needed to construct this new trail was quickly procured, and club members immediately began cutting the area's first second-class trail.

EARLY YEARS

From Rope Tows to Ski Jumps

It was not my intention to build so long a tow, but some members of the ski club persuaded me to run very near the top of the mountain.
—Ted Cooke, designer of the Gunstock Ski Hoist

The construction of a second-class trail in Gilford paved the way for Massachusetts designer Ted Cooke to install a rope tow on the back of Gunstock Mountain in 1935. Given the name Gunstock Ski Hoist, at 3,100 feet it was reported to be the longest tow in the world. It became the country's second rope tow, the first being located in Woodstock, Vermont.

Cooke designed and assembled the tow's components in Swampscott, Massachusetts, in the shops of the Lynn Sand and Stone Company. They were later transported to Gilford, and in the fall of 1934, ground preparation began under the direction of Frank Bacon, a local farmer, and Belknap County commissioner Fred Weeks, an avid skier. Volunteers cut trees, removed brush and installed thirty return rope pulleys up the west side of Gunstock Mountain. Frank's horses moved the components of the tow up 1,100 feet to where a four-cylinder engine had been positioned. From there, his oxen team, Florence and Ted, moved the 6,200 feet of rope to the top of the towline, which sat just below the summit of the mountain. By late January 1935, the tow was complete and ready for use.[3]

In an interview with the *Laconia Evening Citizen*, Ted Cooke reflected on his appreciation for having been involved in the growth of skiing in the Lakes Region:

> *I built my equipment here in Swampscott and trucked it to Gilford. I located there at the invitation of the White Mountain Ski Runners and located on the property of Mr. and Mrs. Weeks and Frank Bacon.*
>
> *We ended up with 6,200 feet of rope which was far longer than anybody has since attempted to operate. We were very short of horse power the first year…*
>
> *The following year we put up a much larger engine and built a house over the rig for comfort and repairs. Three or four years later I built a smaller tow which ran from Batch's barn up to the big tow…I had a lot of fun being a pioneer and gained a great deal of experience.*[4]

The tow offered skiers a strenuous, challenging and sometimes frightening ride up the mountain. When conditions were good, the tow could carry four people at the same time at about thirty miles per hour, taking them on a brisk ride to the top. The rope was heavy, and warm conditions would cause too much slack. Twice a day, an hour-long break was required to remove sections of the rope to correct the problem.

After the first season of use, many improvements appeared in time for the 1936 ski season. Thousands of feet of rough-cut lumber had been carried in to improve rough terrain. The four-cylinder engine was replaced with a bigger six-cylinder, and a wooden structure was constructed to protect the engine from the harsh elements. A forty-foot tower was erected to correct the issue with slack in the rope. Now twice as many people could ride the tow.

This new way to ascend the mountain proved to be wildly popular. The Winnipesaukee Ski Club not only utilized the tow but also ran and supervised its operation. Members of the Appalachian Mountain Club would arrive and meet at the home of Fred Weeks and then stay at Weeks Cabin, a modest home composed of a living room, a waxing room and two bedrooms. The house could easily accommodate up to ten or more people. Boston's White Mountain Ski Runners ran its own cabin for guests, and however simple, it also had its own waxing room.

Ralph Batchelder and his wife had already purchased the old, run-down Copp farm located near the base of the rope tow. The barn, which sat beside a dilapidated farmhouse, was renovated by Ralph into a cabin with two large rooms. It was a primitive structure yet it had electricity. The Batchelders served hearty, home-cooked meals from their home, and the place became affectionately known as Batch's Barn.

The Boston-based White Mountain Ski Runners played a major role in the development of skiing in the Lakes Region. *Courtesy of Gunstock Area Commission.*

Skiing and the operation of the rope tow appeared to run smoothly, at least at first. However, with the ever-increasing number of skiers and the rope tow in full swing, the need for first aid quickly became apparent. While skiing near the tow one weekend, a fourteen-year-old boy lost control, crashed into a tree and broke his ankle. Transportation of the injured boy included a ride down the trail in a toboggan to the Weeks farm and then a trip via an ambulance to the hospital in Laconia. Dr. John R. Parley, the physician treating the patient, was one of the first in the area to suggest having first aid available for skiers on-site. The idea of having an ambulance waiting at the Weeks farm during peak skiing times became an item of discussion between the Laconia Chamber of Commerce and the Laconia chapter of the American Red Cross.

The liability of using a rope tow forced operators to constantly monitor skier injuries. Safety devices installed on the Gilford tow were very primitive and did not appear to have helped much in terms of preventing injuries. A well-known feature installed near the upper bull wheel known as the bang board consisted of a four-inch-thick plank made from sturdy oak with a hole drilled through for the rope. If skiers didn't let go of the rope in time and get their coats, gloves or mittens well clear, they could be guaranteed of an assault by this piece of lumber.

Downhill skiing was put into the same liability category as a roller coaster, and ski jumping was considered off the scale in terms of liability. Savvy ski tow operators realized that selling day tickets created too many opportunities for liability and would only sell single lift tickets. Tickets could only be purchased at the top of the tow, so if an injury occurred on the way up, the attendant knew not to sell the skier a ticket.

Gilford's popular rope tow fueled the increasing popularity of skiing and created quite a distraction for ski enthusiasts. However, the hunt for a new location for a ski jump never stopped, as the area had now been without one for several years. After considerable scouting and surveying by the Winnipesaukee Ski Club, White Mountain Ski Runners, University of New Hampshire and the Eastern Amateur Ski Association, a location on Mount Rowe in Gilford was chosen. The groups searched in several different states but returned to Gilford after it was determined that the terrain on the east side of the mountain could not be more naturally suited for a ski jump. The

The construction of a sixty-meter ski jump on Mount Rowe created jobs in the Lakes Region during the Great Depression. *Courtesy of Gunstock Area Commission.*

Eastern Amateur Ski Association wanted this jump to be the hill it used for all of its eastern championship meets.

In March 1935, the *Laconia Evening Citizen* announced in a short article that a ski jump would be constructed on Mount Rowe at a total cost of $18,000. Many individuals and politicians and all three Belknap County commissioners sought funds from the Federal Emergency Relief Administration (FERA), citing that the project would immediately put at least eighty men back to work.[5]

It was estimated that the project would take three months to complete, and the total number of men being employed would quickly increase to three hundred, with many coming from Boston. Federal funds for its construction were quickly appropriated, and work on the jump, now known as FERA Project No. 2018, officially began on April 3, 1935.

THE CREATION OF THE BELKNAP MOUNTAINS RECREATION AREA

Therefore, when we build, let us think that we build for ever. Let it not be for the present delight, nor for the present use alone; let it be such work as our descendants will thank us for, and let us think, as we lay stone on stone, that a time is to come when those stones will be held sacred because our hands have touched them, and that men will say as they look upon the labor and wrought substance of them, "See! This our fathers did for us." For, indeed, the greatest glory of a building is not in its stones, or in its gold. Its glory is in its Age.

—John Ruskin

The words of John Ruskin must have been swirling through the minds of the men who created the plans for the new ski jump. Soon afterward, the very same men mapped out something far more grand and magnificent: a year-round recreation area built around that single ski jump. Discussions, planning and negotiations for the development of the Belknap Mountains Recreation Area were underway well before the construction of the jump began in 1935. Belknap County commissioners Arthur Rollins, Joseph Smith and John Morrison were working closely with members of their governing body, the Belknap County Legislative Delegation. The commissioners were present at many hearings held at the statehouse in Concord. They were there for one purpose: to urge the development of a major recreation area in Gilford.

The Hussey Manufacturing Company of North Berwick, Maine, was hired to design the jump and recreation facilities, as well as oversee its construction. A committee was formed to assist Hussey chief engineer Lawrence "Ed" Willey through the rough spots in the design of not only the sixty-meter jump but also two more jumps, a forty- and a twenty-meter. The committee was made up of a small group of men, all being extremely knowledgeable in the sport of skiing. Committee members included Harry Wade Hicks of Lake Placid, Dr. Godfrey Dewey and Charles A. Proctor of Dartmouth College, who had been a member of the 1932 Olympic Ski Committee.

One of the primary goals of this massive undertaking was to keep the employed men busy at all times. To do this, as many supplies as possible were to be gathered from the land, even if it proved to be more costly. Stones from the local quarry and lumber cut from the forestland built the entire recreation area. Even the hardware was made on-site by a blacksmith in a small building constructed just for that purpose.

Belknap County purchased almost 135 acres on the northeasterly side of the Belknap Mountain Range on which the jump was to be located. A

The artistry and quality workmanship used to create the recreation area are evident in this stone bridge. *Courtesy of Gunstock Area Commission.*

proposal was made for the purchase of an additional 300 acres of land from property owners Phelps, Harris and Sanborn in order to create a parking area for nearly four thousand vehicles. The county had already appropriated money for the land, materials and equipment to be used for the construction of the road leading to the ski jump. The Town of Gilford was in favor of a proposition to fund one-third of the total cost of the project.

In April 1935, legislators visited the jump site. Beforehand, they attended an important meeting held in Gilford just before the vote on a bill to appropriate $16,500 for the construction of the road leading to the jump.[6] Earlier in the week, the Gilford Board of Selectmen had asked the legislators to consider the construction of the road to be included as a state project.

The meeting began with a lively lunch at the Winnipesaukee Farm, a local inn owned by G. Elmer Sanborn. In attendance were thirty men, including two state senators, members of the Appropriations and the Public Improvements Committees of the New Hampshire House, the three Belknap County commissioners and adjacent property owners.

Once lunch was completed, Captain Edward Lydiard, considered one of the most enthusiastic pioneers in the sport of skiing, gave a brief history of skiing in this area beginning with the formation of the Winnipesaukee Ski Club. He further explained that the rapid growth of skiing here was quickly surpassing sled dog racing in popularity and had firmly placed the Lakes Region in the limelight. Ski manufacturers could not keep up with the demand for equipment, and the State Publicity Bureau was struggling to produce enough ski trail maps.

He told of how the officials of the Eastern Amateur Ski Association had declared the site in Gilford the location for the greatest ski jump in the East. It had explored many sites in several different states but came back to Gilford, stating that nature had provided the best possible hill for a jump. He then stressed the importance for good roads leading to the jump.

The group then took a ride on the back-of-the-mountain road, as it was called, and had to abandon the cars in favor of walking because of the poor condition of the road. As the men walked to the jump site, they soon discovered that much of the land leading up to the jump was swampy and that a brook was being redirected. They then came upon workers who were clearing trees from the jump's landing hill. Large stakes had already been driven into the area of the hill by engineers.

Early work on the landing hill of the big jump included stakes being strategically placed by engineers. *Courtesy of Gunstock Area Commission.*

Waiting to greet them was Ed Willey, the brilliant twenty-six-year-old engineer from Hussey. He and Herman Olsen, Gilford's police chief and superintendent of the recreation area, were on hand with blueprints to answer questions and explain the future development of the area. Both men boasted that Gilford's sixty-meter ski jump was patterned after the famous ski jump in Lake Placid but that the Belknap jump would be one full meter longer.

The members of the group were highly impressed with the project; some were even brave enough to climb the steep landing hill. They became enthusiastic supporters of the project, and when it came time for them to vote on the bill for the appropriation of funds for the road to the jump, it easily passed.

During the summer, the announcement came that President Roosevelt had given a deadline of September 12, 1935, for the filing of proposed Works Progress Administration (WPA) projects. New Hampshire governor H. Styles Bridges immediately appealed to WPA officials. Out of the $2 million available for state projects, he requested funding for both the state road and the jump.

The projects were quickly approved by the president. Funds for the state road arrived soon after, but the ski jump project was held in limbo. The situation became tense when a telegram arrived from the Treasury Department in Washington demanding that all work on the jump stop immediately. County Commissioner Arthur Rollins and Fred Coleman, the director of WPA operations in the state, headed a delegation selected to approach New Hampshire senator Frederick Brown and WPA director William P. Fahey. The men demanded an explanation from the federal government as to the reason for the telegram.

Commissioner Rollins explained that the steel required to construct the ski jump had already been purchased. Neither the senator nor the director could explain why the order to stop all work was issued. Senator Brown assured the men that he would do everything he could in Washington to help with the problem. He kept his promise, and by mid-October the project was back on track after it was discovered that paperwork technicalities had caused the application for funds to be rejected.

Once WPA funding was approved, the Belknap Mountains Recreation Area became known as Project No. 313. The plan for the recreation area now included far more than just the three ski jumps. Continuous additions took place: ski trails, various structures, a recreation building, a skating rink and a toboggan run were all included in the latest design. Future management of the recreation area was often discussed, but no decision was made as to who would run the facility once it was complete.

Most of the work during construction was done by hand using axes and saws, which made cutting through heavily wooded areas slow and difficult. Dynamite was used on the particularly stubborn areas of ledge, which was found in abundance on the property. Concrete was mixed on-site and transported by wheelbarrow. Workers' earnings averaged just over ten dollars per week. Not good pay even then, but every employed man was more than happy to have work.

Their work was so impressive that Governor Bridges announced in March that the state would confer with Charles A. Proctor in reference to placing a bid for the 1940 Winter Olympics. He was hoping that the games would be held at the new recreation center in Gilford. He went so far as to attend Gilford's Old Home Day during August 1936 to announce that an invitation had been made to hold the Olympics at Belknap.[7] Unfortunately, despite a gallant effort, the Olympics never came to the Lakes Region.

By the end of December 1936, the sixty-meter jump was on schedule to be finished by the following February. The toboggan chute was complete and ready to use. Stone Bar, a novice trail, was open and could be skied on with as little as four inches of snow. Also finished was Try-Me, a gentle and winding beginner's slope. Cobble Mountain, standing at 1,388 feet and located immediately on the left after the main entrance, had been entirely cleared. It would take two full years to be completed.

The steep, nameless slalom course was not yet fully finished but could be used with a foot or more of snow. The trail was quickly named after Fletcher Hale, a graduate of Dartmouth and an attorney residing in Laconia. An extremely civic-minded man, he fully supported the promotion of winter sports in the Lakes Region and was a U.S. congressman from the state's first district from 1925 until his untimely death from a bout of pneumonia in 1931.

With steady progress being made, a Tourade was organized by the chamber of commerce in Laconia.[8] In an area-wide celebration, local residents, inns and lodges threw open their doors to the hundreds who gathered at Eagle Square in Laconia. On hand to answer questions were Philip Hussey, Ed Willey, Captain Edward Lydiard—in his new position as development director of the recreation area—WPA officials, county commissioners and members of the Winnipesaukee Ski Club. The jumps, fine trails and recent developments were featured, and the announcement was made that the sixty-meter jump would be finished by February. Philip Hussey also described another project undertaken by his company: the world's largest jump in Berlin, New Hampshire, which Hussey was building for Alf Halvorsen, head of the Nansen Ski Club.

Herman Olsen was on hand to explain that 85 percent of the recreation area had been completed, with WPA funds totaling $300,000 being spent to date. Belknap County had spent far less than one-third of that amount on the project. Olsen called it the largest and most elaborate year-round paradise for sporting enthusiasts. As predicted, almost three hundred men were now employed and working on the project. A request for additional funding for future developments had been filed with the WPA with proposals including a community house, a one-mile bobsled run, two ski tows and a ten-meter jump.[9]

The jump was completed on time and was in perfect condition for the very first competitive meet scheduled at the end of February 1937. The competition, the Eastern Amateur Ski Association Combined Jumping and

Area superintendent Herman Olsen, *left*, takes a break with Foreman Bill O'Connor. *Courtesy of Gunstock Area Commission.*

Cross-Country Championship, was advertised as the greatest event since the 1932 Olympics, and it aroused interest throughout the Northeast. Boston attorney Park Carpenter took one month off from work to run the meet, and those attracted included the best of the field, such as national champion Alf Engen, Sverre Kolerud, the Satre brothers, Sigmund Ruud, Bob Jewett of Dartmouth College, Ernest Dion of Lebanon and local favorite, Emile Levasseur of Laconia.

Due to a lack of snowfall, four hundred tons of ice was flaked to cover the jump for its first meet. The Metropolitan Ice Company of Somerville, Massachusetts, arrived several days ahead to survey the situation. Using two large grinding machines, it took three full days to flake the frozen cubes. Fortunately, a small amount of snow fell during the week, allowing the cross-country portion of the meet to go on as scheduled. That trail system was designed by the meet's chief of course, Edward Blood, also ski coach at the University of New Hampshire.

From the first time ski jumping appeared in 1937, it remained a beloved tradition at the Belknap Mountains Recreation Area. *Courtesy of Gunstock Area Commission.*

Every available room in every hotel, motel and inn was booked. Thousands flocked to the Lakes Region by snow train, car and bus. A special snow train arrived in Laconia on Saturday morning, and more than a dozen buses transported the hordes of people to the recreation area. Over ten thousand spectators arrived, and the parking area was jammed with nearly two thousand cars.

Just before the meet, the jump needed to be tested for the first time. The young man given the honor of taking the first flight from the impressive structure was William Halverson, a Berlin High School student. He was also the son of Alf Halverson of the Nansen Ski Club in Berlin, who happened to be one of the ski jumping judges for the competition.

On Sunday, February 28, 1937, the Belknap Mountains Recreation Area was officially dedicated moments before the competition began. The newly crowned Queen of the Eastern Snows, Miss Ruth McMann, cut away the ribbon that then allowed the number one rated jumper, Carl Holmstrom, to make a perfect sixty-two-meter jump.[10] More than seventy top ski jumpers from around the world competed, with a strong showing by the jumpers from Dartmouth. However, Norway's Sigmund Ruud became the new eastern jumping champion, and his fellow countryman, Sverre Kolterud, came in second. The meet came to an official close with a triple jump made by top jumpers Kenneth Kempe, Carl Holmstrom and Hans Strand.

During the following summer and fall, additional WPA funds became available, and the project progressed quickly. The deluxe chairlift ascending Mount Rowe was under construction. Parking lanes were built to accommodate well over one thousand cars and numerous parking areas for buses were finished. Seven fieldstone fireplaces had been erected. The largest was the Jumbo, which could cook hundreds of clams at once and keep just as many people warm.

During ski season, at Batch's Barn on the back of Gunstock Mountain, skiers were still swarming the slopes. Improvements were made to the old rope tow and to the barn, including new plumbing and shower facilities. The Corkscrew and Winnipesaukee Trails were constantly in use. In another part of Gilford, the King's Grant Inn on Kimball Road ran a rope tow on its gentle slopes and hosted well-attended skiing parties.

It appeared that any slight elevation in the smallest of places saw the addition of a rope tow and skiers. The Lakes Region was in the process of a total transformation. As work progressed on the WPA project and the facilities there grew, it gave the smaller ski operators a run for their money. The Belknap Mountains Recreation Area was slowly reaching its goal of becoming a major sports center in the region.

THE HUSSEY MANUFACTURING COMPANY'S GIFT TO THE LAKES REGION

In some manner, the word got around that we knew quite a bit about ski area development—it may have been that we had more ambition than actual knowledge.
–Philip W. Hussey Sr., Hussey Manufacturing Company

The Hussey Manufacturing Company, builder of the Belknap Mountains Recreation Area, has a long and fascinating history of its own. With the sixth generation of the Hussey family now running the corporation, it celebrated its 175th anniversary in 2010, a testament to the expertise with which its management has skillfully guided it through some of the most difficult times in American history.

The company's history book, *A Long Furrow Plowed*, was written by Philip W. Hussey for the 125th anniversary in 1960. An updated version was printed in 1995 by one of his sons, Philip Jr., and a third edition was written in 2010 by a grandson, Timothy B. Hussey. Within the pages of the book, Philip described in an honest and straightforward manner the early structure of his family's company as being in a continuous search for a reason to be. There was no focus and no real product line, and its only mission was simply to stay in business.

The first product ever produced by the Hussey family was a farm plow featuring a new and innovative design. The American plow was an invention with an incredibly slow evolution, but it was thrown into a completely new arena by William Hussey in 1835. The improvements made to this basic farm tool quickly gained the company international recognition and made work on American farms far more efficient than it ever had been before.

Much is written in the book about Timothy Hussey, a man with great empathy for his fellow man, who carried his company through good and bad times, treating his employees as he would his family. This trait has been passed through the generations and is one of the reasons for the company's success and survival throughout its struggles.

Philip W. Hussey Sr. (1891–1985). *Courtesy of Peter A. Hussey.*

It was Timothy who was leader of the successful enterprise when an all-consuming fire on January 11, 1895, engulfed his family's business. In less than an hour, the entire plant burned down, with more than one thousand pieces of farm equipment, finished and ready to be shipped, being lost. Timothy, then sixty-four years old, decided to turn what was left of the business over to his three sons.

The Hussey family have always believed that the trials and tribulations of life could and should be met head on and with a positive attitude. Such a devastating fire would have meant the end for most businesses; instead, it became a shining example of how to have something extraordinary blossom out of something so devastating.

Timothy's sons put tremendous effort into rebuilding the company and eventually split it into two divisions; one part manufactured plows and farm equipment, while the other focused on the business of building fire escapes.

The second division of the company continued to grow even through the Great Depression and eventually manufactured anything steel: stepladders, sewer grates, manhole covers, park benches and basketball backstops. A department was created and named Winter Sports Engineers and was put to work specifically on the Belknap Mountains Recreation Area. With no experience building ski areas, the company was able to capture the contract for the construction of Gilford's new recreation facility. Its talented and energetic chief engineer, Ed Willey, was put in charge of managing the development of the facility. Philip explained how he and the company didn't hesitate to embrace the project:

> *In Gilford, New Hampshire, the local ski club desired to improve their operations by building a new ski jump. They were able to get the government to sanction the taking over of a sizable acreage of land in the Belknap Mountains and under the WPA arrangement to develop a new*

Ed Willey (left) confers with Fred Coleman, the director of WPA operations for the State of New Hampshire. *Courtesy of Gunstock Area Commission.*

> *winter sports area, with the Board of County Commissioners as the local sponsoring agent...I was called to Gilford and at the end of the day, we here at Hussey were committed to the County Commissioners to design the complete development and to oversee all of the construction under the WPA operations...The project lasted for over three years, with Ed Willey, our engineer in charge living right in the vicinity. Before completion, Ed laid out several miles of black topped roads, a big parking area, several bridges, a big and attractive club house designed here in our office by a young engineer named Mitchell Dirsa. Also included were a complete water supply system, a sanitary system, three ski jumps, one of the 60-meter size, and one of the first chair lifts in this part of the country. It carried skiers to the top of one of the mountains. In fact, when finished, it was one of the finest complete developments in the East and is now enjoyed by thousands each winter.*[11]

Entries in Philip's personal diaries from 1936 show that he attended weekly meetings in Gilford and consulted with Ed Willey quite often. The location of the bobsled run was changed several times. Philip met with Dr. Godfrey Dewey and Harry Wade Hicks of Lake Placid regarding the run before a final decision was made on its design. Further entries show Fred Coleman from the WPA spending most of the day at Philip's office in North Berwick in July 1936 as they met with Ed Willey and Mitchell Dirsa. The four men had the job of trying to figure out how to spend an additional $300,000 on the ski jump project.

Philip became an icon at the company, in part thanks to his incredible leadership and integrity. He turned over the company to his two sons, Philip Jr. and Peter, in August 1967, and by the time he finally stepped down, he had been involved with the company for sixty-four years.

Today Hussey is a leader in stadium and telescoping spectator seating; Hussey seating can be found at the Toronto Skydome; the Joe Robbie Stadium in Miami, Florida; and the Arrowhead Pond of Anaheim in Anaheim, California. The Lakes Region was once again visited by the Hussey Corporation when it installed the seating systems in the gyms and auditoriums of its schools, yet another market benefiting from its products.

The Hussey family throughout the company's existence has always been mindful of its history and obtained the company's original building, which is listed on the National Register of Historic Places. Located adjacent to the corporate offices in North Berwick, it houses the Hussey Family Museum.

The Hussey Family Museum in North Berwick, Maine, is housed in the company's original building. *Photo by author.*

The warm and inviting museum displays a vast collection of items gathered by the family for the past 176 years, including farm plows, small scale models of products and photographs.

The Lakes Region is fortunate to have had this international corporation leave behind a piece of its history here in Belknap County. The company's talent, quality workmanship and ability to rise to a challenge have now become an integral part of the heritage of the recreation area and of New Hampshire.

TRANSFORMATION

Farming to Recreation

The ski area permanently changed the Lakes Region from a farming community to one of recreation. That's why George Ames founded the historical society in Gilford in 1943—he saw farming and its history quickly disappearing.
–Diane Mitton, curator for Gilford's Thompson-Ames Historical Society

Additional WPA funds continued to be appropriated for the further development of the Belknap Mountains Recreation Area, and the local economy began to shift into an environment of recreation. Snow trains from Boston were now transporting more than three thousand passengers to Laconia on a single Sunday. Local residents had no choice but to change how they viewed the harsh New England winters. The long, cold months of December through March became a season to celebrate, not one to hibernate, and the era of the winter carnival was fully embraced. The slogan for the recreation area was "The Spot for Sports." It was marketed as a playground for all seasons, and it became known simply as "the Area."

The growth and changes underway at the Area were being mirrored in the local community. With the large influx of visitors, new inns and lodges began to spring up to accommodate the incoming guests needing a place to stay. One of the most unique lodges in the area opened in early December 1936. The Baraks was built to offer first-class accommodations for skiers and was conveniently located just down the road from the main entrance of

Located near the ski area, the Baraks was built as a first-class ski lodge. *Courtesy of Dick and Maurine Bastille.*

the recreation area.[12] Rough-cut lumber was used to side both the interior and exterior walls, giving it a warm and rustic appearance. Furnishings were simple, with bunks upstairs and a large fieldstone fireplace placed in a central location within the open room downstairs. Present at the grand opening were Belknap County commissioners Joseph Smith, John Morrison and Arthur Rollins. Smith's contribution to the ski lodge was the rough-cut siding processed at his own mill.

In Laconia, guests utilized the Laconia Tavern, an establishment also used by the Winnipesaukee Ski Club for its meetings. In August 1937, a guest staying at the tavern was Christian A. Lund, a native of Norway. Lund owned and operated two companies, Minnesota's Northland Ski Manufacturing Company and the C.A. Lund Company. The companies were turning out both high-end and run-of-the-mill skis along with toboggans, hockey sticks, snowshoes and water skis.

Lund was in the area as a guest of his New England sales representative who was trying to woo his boss and convince him to locate a manufacturing plant in Laconia. After spending one day in the Lakes Region, which included a local scenic flight and boat rides around Lake Winnipesaukee, he was completely sold. By mid-August, he had signed an agreement to build a plant in Laconia, which would bear the name Northland. Laconia banks jumped at the chance to give the company a mortgage. Local officials and businessmen rejoiced at the news, calling it the biggest boon to the city in decades.

One of the many machines used to make wooden skis at Laconia's Northland Ski Company. *Courtesy of Bob Bolduc.*

Lund's sons, Carl and Ambrose, were both ski jumpers, and Carl agreed to stay in the city to oversee the construction of the plant and later run the company. Skiing great Hannes Schneider was hired as a technical advisor. One year later, the manufacturing plant was employing one hundred locals and turning out well over 250 pairs of hickory skis per day.

An employee of the factory, Fred Nachbaur, was helping his parents establish the family-run Arlberg Inn in Gilford. Formerly a farm, the inn had its grand opening in October 1937, and it couldn't have been located in a better place: directly across from the main entrance of the Area. A restaurant was later added, and the establishment was always a favorite gathering spot for skiers.

Fred somehow found enough spare time to run the Winnipesaukee Ski School at the recreation area during 1937 and 1938 and became one of the first certified ski instructors in the country. The initial ski instructors hired by

Once a farmhouse, the Arlberg Inn became a favorite location of many social gatherings for skiers. *Courtesy of Gunstock Area Commission.*

the school were Austrian Sig Vogel and Herbert Bertram, who was destined to become manager at Cannon Mountain in northern New Hampshire. A new trail, named Viking, was constructed for the school to keep beginners away from the more aggressive, experienced skiers.

The Winnipesaukee Ski School moved to the slope behind the Baraks after the bid for the Area's ski school was lost to Earle Chandler in 1939. The new leader brought in instructors Fred Noseworthy and Ken Boothroyd, the former head of the ski patrol at Cannon Mountain. The school ran popular weekly slalom races and arranged for Carl Lund of the Northland Ski Company to serve as an official.

The all-season single chairlift on Mount Rowe was installed and officially dedicated in February 1938. A large group of WPA workers, numbering in the hundreds, had been engaged in keeping the project on track to meet the completion date. This novel new way to ascend a mountain drew even greater numbers to the recreation spot and had just as many passengers during the off-season as it did during a typical ski season.

The first chairlift in the East, located on Mount Rowe, was an all-season lift. *Courtesy of Gunstock Area Commission.*

Just before the championship meet of 1938, the Winnipesaukee Ski Club hosted its annual ski ball. More than five hundred attended the lavish affair held at the state armory in Laconia. A small log cabin was constructed and set before a mural depicting a ski country scene with tall pines and a bright blue sky overhead. Refreshments were served from the cabin by club members.

The meet proved to be just as noteworthy. Dartmouth College once again sent a large number of athletes, including Dick Durrance and the Chivers brothers, Howard and Warren. Lebanon Outing Club sent Ernest Dion, and eight cars filled with competitors arrived from Lake Placid. With a fresh coating of snow having fallen the night before, Edward Gignac of Lebanon winged his way to victory. The year before, he had gone unnoticed.

By March, plans for an elaborate yet rustic lodge were being presented to the county commissioners for their approval. Mitchell Dirsa, an architect employed by the Hussey Manufacturing Company, designed the building to complement the rustic appearance of the other structures located throughout the facility. His floor plan included a large kitchen, a huge fireplace made from fieldstones quarried on-site and a first-aid room. The second floor would consist of a continuous balcony running along all four walls that could seat almost five hundred people.

The structure, named the Recreation Building, was under construction when a hurricane in 1938 ripped through New Hampshire in September, leveling acres upon acres of trees across the state. Laborers were immediately sent to work to process the vast amount of lumber that could be obtained from the toppled trees. The historic hurricane lumber was then used in the construction of the building.

By the end of the year, Gordon Langill of the Winnipesaukee Ski Club was proud to announce that the twenty-meter jump was complete. Earle Chandler, ski coach at Laconia High, was the first person to take flight from the new jump. The ten-meter jump was still under construction. Ed Blood, coach of the ski team at the University of New Hampshire, brought his team to the Area to practice and expressed interest in holding some of the school's winter carnival activities there.

The championship meet held in 1939 saw the arrival of the ski jumping phenomenon Torger Tokle; international ski jumping stars also arrived with him. Competitors arriving for the meet included Dartmouth's Dick Durrance and Eric Sand, Art Devlin, Raymond Dion and local jumper Earle Chandler.

Farther away from the jumps and closer to the Recreation Building, a slope named Phelps was in use. The trail had been named after the Phelps family of Gilford from whom some of the land for the Area was purchased. Its eight-hundred-foot rope tow became a popular addition, and the trail was illuminated for skiing at night.[13]

As the development progressed, mistakes were made, and the trail on Cobble Mountain was one of them. The mountain had been clear-cut, which exposed it to high winds. A constant melting and refreezing of the surface left the wide-open trail constantly icy. In 1940, a rope tow was added, and a suggestion was made for trees to be planted to fill in the barren landscape. The challenging conditions proved to be too much, and skiing on this mountain was abandoned shortly after the rope tow was installed.

Another tow in the process of being dismantled was Ted Cooke's original Gunstock Ski Hoist on the back of Gunstock Mountain. Skiers now flocked to Gilford's new and exciting sports facility, and activity on the other side of the mountain became almost nonexistent. The entire tow, therefore, was removed and sold to the Commonwealth Country Club in Boston.

Frank Bacon and his team of oxen, well known for helping to install that historic rope tow, were now at the Area hauling snow to the landing hill of the sixty-meter jump for the championship meet held in March 1940. Jumping stars from all over the world once again made an appearance in the Lakes Region, and it could only be the incredible Torger Tokle who would win the meet.

At the time of the meet, the Recreation Building was about halfway complete. As work progressed, some local taxpayers felt that it was far too extravagant and that a smaller structure would have served the purpose just as well. Hussey's Ed Willey's explanation included the fact that the people who would frequent the recreation area would be of the upscale type and would expect such a building. Once the structure was completed, it became the most expensive WPA structure ever to be constructed in the state.

In Laconia, a new and important ski business had opened. Piche's Ski Shop was owned and run by Francis Piche and his brothers Vincent, Frederick and Eli. Francis was already known in the Lakes Region for being a talented skier and was on the first ski team to be formed at Laconia High School. He went

The Recreation Building, an architectural masterpiece, was built from stones and lumber drawn from the land surrounding it. *Courtesy of Gunstock Area Commission.*

on to become the coach of the Laconia High School Winter Sports Team in 1938.

The Piche brothers ran a small ski shop out of the basement of a house on Merrimac Street and during the off-season maintained a photography studio upstairs. The ski shop was always well stocked with hundreds of skis and accessories, as well as a large selection of tools for repairs. Most of the skis came from the nearby Northland factory, and in addition to offering skis, the brothers were experienced in being able to fit skis properly to skiers, ensuring the safest possible skiing experience.

Skier safety remained a constant consideration for many in the industry. After the opening of the Area, the Winnipesaukee Ski Club put out a call for one of its members to step up and organize a ski patrol. Harold J. Piper answered the call of duty and became the first leader of the Belknap Mountain Red Cross Ski Patrol. He was already busy snapping aerial images of the ski area and had a fine reputation as a professional photographer.

Piper's group had high standards and its purpose was to prevent accidents, yet the members were trained to handle the injured should an accident

The original Piche's Ski Shop was started in the home of expert skier Francis Piche. *Courtesy of Bob Bolduc.*

The need for first aid on the trails became apparent early on in the development of the sport. *Courtesy of Ray Reed.*

occur. Members were assigned specific trails at certain times and were not allowed to leave their trails until other patrolmen relieved them. Patrolmen stayed on duty until the tows were shut down at the end of the day, and each trail was officially shut down by the patrolmen. Detailed reports were made after each accident and reviewed; improvements and suggestions were then made. Materials and supplies used by the patrol were donated by the Laconia chapter of the American Red Cross.

In 1940, Harold received the honor of being made a member of the National Ski Patrol at the end of the ski season. Dozens of letters had been received from doctors, skiers and accident victims describing the exemplary work that he and the members of the patrol had consistently provided on the slopes. Their first-aid work was professional and prevented further injury, and all was done with a cheerful manner. Skiers made note of their presence and appreciated the fact that members were always there to help if required.

The Belknap Mountains Recreation Area was now on its way to completion, and every aspect of the facility—whether it was the sixty-meter

The sixty-meter jump and the recreation area built around it became the Lakes Region's pride and joy. *Courtesy of Bob Bolduc.*

jump, the first chairlift in the East or the unsung heroes of the ski patrol who took care of the injured—was of the highest quality. The impressive recreation area became the pride and joy of the Lakes Region.

However, big changes were looming on the horizon. With the war in Europe escalating, the government needed more funds for its defense, and any further WPA funding for the project was halted. Many of the ideas and hopes for the recreation area were left in the blueprint stage, but with a vibrant facility that boasted a total price tag of $1 million, both the transformation of the Lakes Region and Gunstock's legacy of excellence had begun.

TORGER TOKLE

Norway's Legendary Ski Sensation and America's Adopted Son

I have fond memories of the 1941 ski jumping competition at that jump. Watching Torger Tokle and the other competitors flying through the air off that huge, towering structure was a brand-new experience for me. I was only six at the time and, of course, did not fully appreciate what I was seeing, but it was probably the most spectacular event of my very young life. I remember that the crowd was extremely enthusiastic in expressing their appreciation for the demonstration, with talk of a world's record jump, perhaps, by the "fabulous" Torger Tokle.

–Dave Roberts, historian and avid hiker of the Belknap Mountain Range

Torger Dahl Tokle, with his big smile, irrepressible optimism and good-natured approach to life burst onto the scene of American ski jumping in 1939. Lacking appropriate words to describe this young phenomenon, the press simply dubbed him a "ski sensation." During the twenty-five years this young man walked and skied on this earth, he accomplished what many of us will never achieve in an entire lifetime.

Torger arrived here as a clean-cut nineteen-year-old, landing in Manhattan during January 1939. Learning to ski as a boy in Norway, by the age of thirteen he had already become a seasoned veteran of jumping exhibitions on the Granasser Hill in his hometown of Lokken Verk.

His brother, Kyrre, also a ski jumper, was scheduled to appear in a competition at Bear Mountain, New York, just a few short hours after his

All of the energy and youthful optimism possessed by Torger shined through his irrepressible smile. *Courtesy of Kenneth Tokle.*

sibling had taken his first steps onto American soil. Brand new to this country and only able to speak a few words of English, Torger expressed to Kyrre that he, too, wanted to "yump."[14]

Yump he did, and he never once looked back. During his first day in New York, on a pair of borrowed skis, he entered the competition as a Class B jumper, bested all classes of jumpers and set a new hill record at Bear Mountain. He was promptly moved into the elite, Class A group of jumpers.

It didn't take him long to appear on the jumping scene at Belknap. While at the eastern championship held there on March 4, 1939, Torger was already rated as a top jumper. Both he and Reidar Andersen, one of the best jumpers in the world at the time, tied for first, setting a dual hill record of 220 feet. Andersen admitted before the competition that he had never heard of the newcomer. Not many had.

In an instant, the fellow with the unforgettable name became a favorite with the ski editor of the *New York Times*, Frank Elkins. The bright young Norwegian quickly became easier to interview, for with the help of night school he quickly mastered the English language. During one of those interviews with Elkins, Torger included jumping off the sixty-meter jump at Belknap as one of his most exciting moments. Calling it "his hill," he believed that the jump was one of the finest, if not *the* finest, in this country.

Torger Tokle was able to do for the sport of ski jumping what no other athlete since has been able to do for any sport—and all in a matter of four years. He won first place at almost every meet and consistently broke one hill record after another. He became the U.S. national champion in 1941, the same year he set the long-standing record at the sixty-meter jump in Gilford. In total, he won forty-two of the forty-eight sanctioned tournaments in which he competed.

Torger enjoyed immense popularity and quickly became a favorite with photographers. *Courtesy of Gunstock Area Commission.*

During the off-season, he earned his livelihood as a carpenter, first building docks at the Brooklyn Navy Yard in New York. From there it was on to building the bulkhead along the East River Drive. When asked if his exercise program was structured to get him in shape for jumping season, he laughed at the notion, saying that he got more than enough exercise at his job to keep him in shape. A far higher salary could have easily been his had he become a ski instructor, but he had no interest in giving up his amateur status as a jumper in order to make more money.

His disposition was gentle and unassuming, yet it was his nature to be a fierce competitor. Considering all competitors his friends, the ever-friendly Norwegian would say with a hearty handshake when greeting them, "It seems just like getting home to be back in Laconia with you boys."[15] His arrival at the scene of championship meets was quiet and unheralded by any fanfare. This was something so unique and intriguing to the public and the press, and it made this celebrity even more of a champion in their eyes.

Ski jumping was not the only sport enjoyed by the young, gifted Torger. *Courtesy of Kenneth Tokle.*

In 1940, he was favored to win the meet at Belknap, and the press insisted that it was possible for him to break his own hill record of 220 feet that he had set one year earlier. Becoming known for his power leaps and unerring form, he did indeed break the record with a leap of 235 feet. The meet brought a spectacular close to his competitive schedule for the season.

In competitions leading up to the 1941 championship meet at Belknap, the star athlete smashed hill records left and right. He broke a hill record at Lake Placid that had stood for nine years and was considered unbreakable. From this he went to Brattleboro and set the hill record there as well.

The day before the meet in the Lakes Region, headlines across the country shouted the news that the event at the Belknap Mountains Recreation Area had turned into a nationwide spectacle. The *Laconia Evening Citizen* filled its pages with articles about the champion, his competitors and the sport of ski jumping. Reporters described him as, "not having changed from the smiling pleasant young man who was here last year, who was gracious to all, kindly to the children who flocked around him, firm in his determination to give the public a spectacle of record-breaking ski jumping, supreme in his quiet confidence that he can and will do just that."[16]

He arrived in Laconia with his brother early on Friday, March 7, his twenty-second birthday. The brothers spent the morning working on the landing hill, preparing it for the big meet two days later. Reporters followed his every move and compared his levelheadedness as a celebrity to Rudyard Kipling's poem "If," describing him as being of fine character.

The highly anticipated meet was opened by New Hampshire governor Robert O. Blood with over seven thousand enthusiastic spectators in attendance, all braving a windy snowstorm. The field of competitors was the largest since the eastern meets first began in 1922, with jumping stars Art Devlin, Jay Rand, Ottar Satre, Ed Gignac and Carl Holmstrom being some of the top names listed on the roster. Torger fully intended to win and was heard to say that he was going to bring home the Winnipesaukee Trophy so that his grandchildren could admire it fifty years down the road.

This time, not on a pair of borrowed hickories but rather on a pair of his own Northlands, he flew far beyond the safety mark of the hill, as well as all of the measurers, who wondered where he had gone. Falling out of the sky, he landed almost on one ski onto the transition to the flat of the hill, the impact causing his skis to sink almost four inches into the snow. His massive leap was 39 feet farther than the landing point of his nearest competitor, setting a new hill record of 251 feet. This new record became his seventeenth. The quiet, humble, ever-popular young lad had just become known as "our champion" to the residents of the Lakes Region.

The next day, when returning to the scene of his record jump, he laughed and said, "If I knew how far I was going, I would never have looked for more distance!"[17] He admitted that his snow glasses had fogged up on takeoff and that he had no idea where he was going but figured that his skis would again meet the earth somewhere, somehow. All of his competitors had been beaten, including his biggest admirer and close friend Art Devlin, whose leaps fell far short of the champion's. The Winnipesaukee Trophy had easily become Torger's.

By the end of 1941, World War II was weighing heavily on the hearts and souls of mankind, and Torger's mind was not focused on his jumping career. He was waiting to be drafted into the United States Army and was also awaiting his citizenship papers. The young man was full of optimism, as was proven by his words during an interview:

> *Germany took over my native country, but it'll never take over my people. When the Government calls me, I'm going to try for the ski troops. I once carried a radio pack down a ski jump and landed right side up, so I don't think I'd have any trouble carrying a gun. They've already taken a lot of my friends who jumped with me last season. Remember Harold Johansen of the Telemark Ski Club? He was the first to go—nearly a year ago.*

> *I'd prefer some competition before being called, then maybe the Army will let me off weekends for other meets later in the year.*[18]

The jumping season of 1942 was the last time he appeared in the Lakes Region. Just days before the meet, he set a new jump record in this country, leaping 289 feet at Iron Mountain, Michigan, in front of more than twenty-five thousand spectators. That jump bettered his previous record by 1 foot, which he set the year before near Seattle, Washington. The skis worn during that record-breaking jump were auctioned off at Rockefeller Center in New York City. Those attending the auction included Crown Prince Olav and Crown Princess Martha of Norway. Proceeds were shared by two organizations to provide relief and comfort to the sea forces and the merchant seamen of the United States and Norway.

During the 1942 championship meet in Gilford, he came in a rare second to Art Devlin. A hearty dinner and rousing celebration were held at the Laconia Tavern that evening, with such greats as Laconia mayor Robinson W. Smith, Alf Halvorsen, Professor Charles A. Proctor, Edward Blood, Gordon Langill and Merrill "Mezzie" Barber in attendance. One of the last things Torger said before leaving was, "Next year I will come early and really prepare the hill, and then you will see some real record breaking."[19]

It was never meant to be. In April of the following year, he was chosen to become a member of the revered Tenth Mountain Division, becoming a citizen of this country the same month. Now fighting for the country he embraced as his own, this new challenge was given as much energy as ski jumping, and he quickly rose to the rank of sergeant.

During an interview in which he revealed his thoughts about becoming an American citizen and fighting in the war, he said:

> *I have many reasons to be glad I have become an American citizen. One is the similarity in ideals and social set-ups between the United States of America and my beloved country, Norway. Also for the stand this nation is taking during the present trying times as the champion of the small and downtrodden nations of Europe. These and many other things have given me the courage and inspiration and filled me with determination to achieve the highest possible. In my particular field of amateur sport, I have had the good fortune to reach the top and in my workaday life, I'm happy and contented.*[20]

He knew that he was at the top of his sport but never failed to mention his younger brother, Arthur, whom he believed was a far superior ski jumper. After being forced from Norway due to the war, Torger had made repeated attempts to bring his brother to this country; all were unsuccessful.

The champion was last mentioned in the *Laconia Evening Citizen* in February 14, 1944, in an article stating that he was stationed at Camp Hale, Colorado, a training camp perched at 9,500 feet above sea level. During a rare bit of recreational time, he entered the Thirty-first Steamboat Springs Winter Sports Carnival, leapt 226 feet and easily won the competition.

By the time his regiment was shipped off to fight in Europe, he had become the closest of friends with journalist Frank Elkins. In a letter later written to him, the skiing star noted, "I'm now on the front and have had contact with the Kraut. I can't tell you much of myself and my job, but we do have quite a bit of snow here, but not much chance of going skiing. When we do go out on skis, it's not the way I prefer to ski."[21]

It was the last letter Elkins would ever receive from him, and it arrived just days before the news of his friend's death. Tragically, Torger was killed during a battle in the Apennines Mountains of Italy on March 3, 1945. He was just twenty-five years old and was four days short of his twenty-sixth birthday.

An article appearing in the March 17, 1945 edition of the *Laconia Evening Citizen* described the heroism of this young leader and his platoon:

> *Sgt. Torger D. Tokle, one of the great skiers of all time, was killed leading his infantry platoon during an attack by the 10th Mountain Division across rugged Apennine Peaks.*
>
> *Shell fragments cut down the 25-year-old ski jumper-soldier shortly after his rifle company of the 86th Regiment jumped off north of the 3300-foot Monte Torraccia in a drive which resulted in an advance of four miles through some of the most rugged terrain of the Apennines.*
>
> *Tokle's platoon was aiming for the little town of Monte Forte, two miles to the north, when a fragment from the heavy concentration of shells the enemy had been pouring on the American positions for days struck and killed him.*
>
> *A platoon leader of Company A of the 86th he and his men aided in the sealing of a tremendous ridge west of the Monte Beivedere which preceded the general attack.*

> *The ridge, five miles long and 3,500 feet high is so sheer the mountaineers had to use fixed ropes and other special peak-climbing equipment to get up its rocky sides. At the top they caught the German garrison completely by surprise, seized the entire mass and held it for three days against repeated desperate Nazi counterattacks.*
>
> *Officers of other units said the feat was one of the most brilliant mountain-climbing operations of this campaign.*

Bill Duncan became good friends with Torger Tokle when the pair lived in Brooklyn, New York, many years before they both landed up in the same regiment of the Tenth Mountain Division. Together they would travel the fifty miles from their hometown to Bear Mountain so they could jump there. Many days were spent together enjoying the company of each other and the sport of ski jumping.

Sadly, Bill fought in the battle that resulted in the death of his friend and was close enough to witness what happened, as he recalled during an interview:

> *Torger always said he was going to join the Tenth Mountain Division. I told him that if he joined, I was going to join also. After that, we lost track of each other for a little while. Well, we both landed up at Camp Hale, Colorado, in the same regiment of the Tenth Mountain Division—and in the same building! We saw each other just about every day. The training there was tough. Every obnoxious thing they could do to us, they did. But every single day of my life I am thankful for that training because it not only got me through what I went through over there, but it got me through everything life has thrown my way.*
>
> *During the battle where Torger was killed, he and Arthur Tokola were pinned down. I was pinned down about one hundred yards from them. I heard artillery and looked up, saw it hit a limb of a tree, bounce off, and explode right over them. When I learned both of them had died, it was a teary time, but we had our orders to keep going and we did; we had to leave them behind. The Italians have a phrase, "Sempre Avanti," which means "always forward," and we used to say that all the time. There is only one thing to do in a situation like that—go forward. You just can't look back.*
>
> *Even now I can't think about that time for too long. Torger was a great guy, and we had great times together.*

Earl Norem, a twenty-year-old member of the Eighty-fifth Regiment of the Tenth Mountain Division, fought alongside Torger's regiment in the Italian Campaign. Fate brought the two men together several times during the highs and lows of life:

> *I was a huge fan of Torger Tokle. He was quite a bit older than I, and my father, being a native of Norway, used to take me to see Torger jump at Bear Mountain, New York, when I was twelve years old. I used to love to watch him jump.*
>
> *I met Torger when I was in the Tenth Mountain Division. We were both sergeants in different regiments, and he taught us how to teach our men hand-to-hand combat. He was very well liked and was always very upbeat.*
>
> *The conditions in the mountains of Italy were much easier than they were when we trained in Colorado. If you could get through the training there, you could do anything; sleeping out in the open when it was forty below wasn't so bad at all. The Germans couldn't figure out how we could run up and down the mountains in Italy, but you see, the mountains in Colorado were much higher, so we were used to the altitude.*
>
> *As we moved through the mountains in Italy, our regiments would leapfrog towards the enemy. We lost so many skiers in that campaign…*
>
> *The next time I saw Torger was when I found his body on the battlefield. He was lying next to his buddy, and they were both facing the enemy. I was one of the men assigned to bring his body down off the mountain, and I cried all the way down…he died a hero.*

As the news of Torger's death reached the States, the nation was left in shock. The country's young people were especially hard hit, as the role model they had idolized had suddenly been snatched away from them forever. The world had lost one of the best athletes it had ever seen, but more importantly, it had lost one of its finest and most noble young men.

It was inconceivable that his death had occurred two months before the unconditional surrender of the Germans. It is understandable, however, with the insurmountable Tenth Mountain Division relentless in its pursuit, that the fearful Germans in Italy surrendered ahead of the general surrender. The end of this brutal war allowed one of Torger's dreams to come true: freedom for his people in Norway. However, his remains were not returned to his beloved homeland; he was buried in Italy, where his life had ended.

It didn't take long for the honors to begin rolling in for the late ski jumping star. By September 1945, at the annual meeting of the Sportsmanship Brotherhood held at the Union League Club in New York City, the following resolution was adopted unanimously: "For his consistent and constant exemplifying of the highest type of sportsmanship as a champion competitor in this great sport of skiing and in all other human relationships, and for his wholesome influence on, and example to, the youth of the world, the Sportsmanship Brotherhood cites, Torger Tokle, to receive its Certificate of Award for Nineteen Hundred and Forty-Four."[22]

In the Lakes Region, an effort was led by Captain Edward Lydiard and the Winnipesaukee Ski Club to gain permission from the Belknap County commissioners to name the sixty-meter jumping hill at Belknap the Torger Tokle Memorial Ski Jump. All three commissioners swiftly and unanimously voted in favor of the request. The jump he had loved so much and considered

Kyrre, Alf and Art Tokle admire their late brother's many trophies displayed at the Bear Mountain Inn in New York. *Courtesy of Kenneth Tokle.*

his hill was named in his memory during a special ceremony on Sunday, March 10, 1946, one year after his tragic death.

A few years later, another one of Torger's dreams came true when his younger brother, Arthur, landed on the shores of America shortly before the championship meet at Belknap in 1948. He was allowed to compete on the hill that now bore the name of his late brother. Torger was right about his little brother—he was an incredible ski jumper and went on to have a long and successful career in the sport of ski jumping in this country.

Honors continued to be awarded to the late ski sensation for years after his tragic death. He was later inducted into the U.S. Ski Hall of Fame in 1959. His little brother once again followed in his big brother's footsteps, becoming an inductee into the Hall of Fame in 1970.

One last piece of the puzzle remained out of place: Torger's burial in Italy. His mother requested that his remains be returned to his beloved country of Norway. It was a request that was granted, and he is now buried in his hometown of Lokken Verk; he had finally come home.

Torger Tokle is a true hero in every sense of the word. He remained noble regardless of what life handed him, from being forced out of his homeland of Norway at such a young age to remaining unchanged by his celebrity status, as well as facing impending doom in order to win the fight against the enemy. The loss of his tremendous potential and thoughts of what he might have become still remain, decades after his death.

Torger D. Tokle (March 7, 1920–March 3, 1945). *Courtesy of Kenneth Tokle.*

GROWING PAINS

The Postwar Years

We should not need to be convinced of the value and potentialities of the Area as a winter playground and as a business asset to this region…we have made an investment…the sole question is whether it is worth protecting and if so, how.

–Laconia attorney Arthur Nighswander, Winter Sports Committee Report to the Belknap County Delegation, December 1944

No bomb needed to be dropped during World War II in order for every fiber of American society to be affected and changed in some way. Rationing and shortages became an accepted way of life. Limited supplies of gasoline and a severe shortage of rubber put an eventual end to all use considered unnecessary, including recreational driving.

By 1940, government WPA funds were being used for the construction of Laconia Airport in Gilford as part of the build-up of the country's defense system. Longtime superintendent of the Area, Herman Olsen, was told by the county commissioners to switch from his present position to one at the airport. Not wanting to leave, he quit. Hussey's Ed Willey moved to the airport project and became the assistant director of WPA operations in the state.

With no funding from the government, the Area was completely on its own. No decisions had ever been made on how to run or fund the project, but the commissioners refused to ask towns to supply tax dollars for its operation or maintenance. The public was in no mood to start supplying funds for the project, anyway—they were focused on the war raging in Europe.

They did, however, take the time to watch international jumping stars compete in the championship meet held in March of that year. The national interest and excitement added a sparkle to the lives of local residents, who were worried about the world at war. The distraction it created was a blessing.

The meet attracted thousands, but it was nowhere near financially successful. The Eastern Amateur Ski Association informed the county that it would not consider Belknap for its competition the following year unless conditions improved. By March 1941, the problems had still not been addressed. Surprisingly, the ski organization did return with its most-anticipated skiing event, the annual cross-country, ski jumping and combined championship meet.

With the competitive season over, the issues that had been ignored were found to be just the beginning of a long list of problems with the conditions at the Area. Shortly after the conclusion of the final meet, the county commissioners created the Chamber of Commerce Winter Sports Committee, appointing Laconia attorney Arthur Nighswander as chairman. The committee acted as a clearinghouse for the public's concerns and suggestions for the facility. While the committee worked on a list of suggestions, good news arrived in October. The Eastern Amateur Ski Association was considering making Belknap a permanent home for its championship meets. Earle Chandler, a member of the Winnipesaukee Ski Club, had been chosen as a delegate to represent the club at the national convention in New York City at the end of the month. His trip was a resounding success. The Belknap Mountains Recreation Area was chosen as the permanent locale for the championship meet, in part because the sixty-meter jump was considered to be one of the best.

One of the first things the Winter Sports Committee did was place an ad with the State Publicity Bureau. The advertising made a tremendous difference; the Area was filled with thousands of skiers during one weekend in February 1942, breaking an all-time record for skier visits. With an abundance of snow, the Phelps rope tow saw a steady stream of activity, buses carrying skiers arrived from Massachusetts and members of the Dartmouth and University of New Hampshire Outing Clubs were out in force on the trails.

Attendance peaked during the championship meet held in March, which fell under the direction of Earle Chandler. The National Ski Association, scheduled to hold its championship meet in California, transferred to Belknap due to the military closing its course on the West Coast. It was the last time some of the jumping stars would compete at Belknap; many left shortly afterward to fight in the war.

The conclusion of the competitive season in 1942 became a turning point for the recreation spot. The war in Europe was progressing at an alarming rate. More and more young men were being called into service. The legality of any government funding of the Area was being questioned, and there was no proof that the funding was even in the best interests and welfare of Belknap County.

Suddenly, the future of the government's investment in the sports facility was unclear and doubtful at best. What had begun as a lifesaving project during the Depression quickly became a target of criticism. The use of taxpayer money to fund its operations became a hotly debated topic.

Seizing on the confusion, a man by the name of Howard Ballou came forward and offered $25,000 for the picturesque park in the Belknap Mountains. It was immediately met with tremendous opposition. The original offer went up to $50,000, and then the hopeful businessman informed the county commissioners that he was prepared to go as high as $125,000.[23]

An emergency meeting of the Laconia Chamber of Commerce was held, and a motion was unanimously passed opposing the sale or lease of the area. Notice of this action was given in writing to the county commissioners, who had received the initial offer, but it was already known that any sale of the area would have to be sanctioned by the legislative delegation.

Adding to the turmoil, New Year's Day 1943 was rung in with the closing of the facility, and all ski competitions were cancelled until the end of the war. As the year dragged on, there was considerable public interest and pressure to have the Area operational for the upcoming ski season. The chairlift was not functional and would not be repaired until the war was over. The commissioners were considering a lease on the Recreation Building, which included its care.

The issue of how to manage the operation was hashed out during a meeting of the Belknap County Legislative Delegation in November 1943. The matter of selling it had met with so much opposition that the delegation did not need to hold a meeting to address the proposal. No amount of discussion seemed to solve the question of its operation.

After much wrangling and planning, the ski season officially opened at the end of November with a fresh snowfall of eighteen inches. With the Area now experiencing some activity, Arthur Nighswander sent a report from the Winter Sports Committee to the delegation outlining his suggestions for improving the conditions for skiers. He respectfully cautioned that perhaps even delegation members did not fully comprehend what this recreation spot had to offer. Anyone he had ever talked with about the facility stated that for all-around advantages there was no other place in this part of the country offering skiing in the winter, a picturesque lake in the summer and mountains with spectacular summit views for hiking. His prediction was that after the war had been won and gas rationing became a thing of the past, a huge resurgence of activity would be witnessed. He also predicted that the general public would be far more demanding than ever before, and he knew that other managers of other winter recreation centers were already planning on how best to attract those crowds to their facilities.

With no insult intended, he further suggested that the operations of the facility should not be in the hands of the three commissioners, who had no training for or understanding of this sort of responsibility. However, his number one criticism of the commissioners was that they did not seek advice, especially from those with more experience with the ski industry. His suggestions included the establishment of a permanent ski school, which would be advertised as part of the permanent facilities at the ski area. He strongly suggested the completion of the forty-meter jump, insisting that it would create more local interest and become an invaluable tool in the training of future jumpers. He also felt a full-time, year-round executive director should be hired. The director needed to be concerned not just with profits but rather focus more on the advertising and promotion of the ski area and fully understand the need to schedule activities in the off-season.

Shortly after the report was delivered, Earle Chandler, head of the ski school, stepped forward and offered the commissioners $100,000 for the property.[24] The commissioners angrily fired back that they had no intention of ever selling the facility. They had been told in no uncertain terms by members of the public that they would be crucified if they sold the property since it belonged to the people and not them. Seeing the strong public sentiment, Chandler swiftly withdrew his offer.

One month later, a bill outlining the operation of the facility was awaiting the review of the county delegation. The bill noted that the Belknap County

Legislative Delegation should take control of the operation of the recreation area and employ a director, and when directed, the director should give back any profits over $10,000 to the delegation. The delegation favored the bill but made it clear that more study was needed before it would vote in favor of it.[25]

When a compromise bill was introduced suggesting a five-member commission to run the Area, no one in the delegation would even second the motion. The county commissioners, therefore, remained in charge of it, with their operations being overseen by the delegation. The employment of a salaried year-round manager was favored, and improvements to the trails and comfort station were recommended.

The manager the commissioners hired was John Proctor, who took over the reins from William Buckley. Despite the weather not always being in his favor, he was able to show an increase in skier visits and revenue. For the first time in years, the future of the Area began to look brighter.

Throughout all of the disagreements and struggles, positive things were happening. In 1947, Bob Montana's *Archie* comic strip characters Archie and Veronica found their way to the ski area in Gilford, and their skiing adventures appeared in the strip. After a ride up the single chairlift and skiing on barrel staves that Archie called "independent pickle packers," he inadvertently found his way onto Fletcher Hale or, more appropriately named by the characters, "Suicide Slope."[26] Shortly after that strip appeared in the papers, Montana brought his new bride to live in the Lakes Region. They moved to Meredith, a town just north of the ski area, where they settled and raised their family.

The Lakes Region experienced another very important arrival just before the 1947 ski season. Bill Trudgeon, formerly of Vermont, moved to the area after falling in love with the landscape and scenery. Bill was a native of Minnesota, began his jumping career in 1935 and was already a familiar face at Belknap jump competitions, first as a member of the Lake Placid Sno Birds and then for the Brattleboro Outing Club. He became employed by the Northland Ski Company in Laconia and quickly impressed the leaders of the Winnipesaukee Ski Club. They did not hesitate to ask him to become their new volunteer coach-manager for the 1947 season.

This move returned the club to the competitive arena, a place it had not been since the country had gone to war. At the height of the war, membership in the club was down to a handful of members, but by the beginning of

1946, membership was hovering at just under one hundred. By 1947, the club was hoping to have at least two hundred members.

Trudgeon immediately saw what others had known for years: the lack of a forty-meter jump was handicapping the training of local jumpers because the transition from the twenty-meter to the sixty-meter was too great. Ten years of dreaming and wishing came to a quick end when Trudgeon secured county funding for the construction of the jump. Even before getting the green light, he and fellow club members were cutting trees and clearing brush on the hill where the jump was to be constructed. The jump was completed in December 1948, and it was officially christened on February 13, 1949. He was, of course, one of the first jumpers to take flight from the newly completed structure.

Also making their first appearance in the late 1940s were the young Dion cousins—Bernie, Doug and Roger. They were members of the Amazing Jumping Dions, along with Bernie's father, Ray, and his uncle, Ernie. Ray

Doug, Roger and Bernie Dion pose with Miss New Hampshire 1950, Miss Betty Laurie. Fritzie Baer appears far right. *Courtesy of Gunstock Area Commission.*

and Ernie were already well known at Belknap and were accomplished athletes. Young Bernie, by the time he was nine years old, had soared from every big hill in the East. The fearless young jumpers captivated crowds and were an expected and highly anticipated part of summer and winter jumping competitions.

The Dions were competitors in the meet that officially signaled the return of the Winnipesaukee Ski Club to annual championships. The competition, held in March 1949, brought nearly two hundred of the top jumping stars from America, Canada and Norway to the sixty-meter jump now named after Torger Tokle. Top-notch American stars included war veteran Art Devlin and Mezzie Barber.

During July, in the blistering heat, one of the most unique events ever to be held at the Area appeared on the forty-meter jump: summer ski jumping. A committee from the Winnipesaukee Ski Club, led by Bill Trudgeon and Fred Nachbaur, coordinated the complex efforts to bring artificial snow to the landing hill of the jump, much to the disbelief of local residents. Sixty tons of ice from the Laconia-Lakeport Ice Company was crushed on site, and tiny particles of ice were spread on the trestle, landing hill and out-run.[27]

It was a work of art to keep the ice from melting in the hot summer sun. Early in the morning before the sun rose on the day of the event, volunteers

Tons of chipped ice were sent down metal chutes in preparation for summer ski jumping on the forty-meter jump. *Courtesy of Bob Bolduc.*

placed straw in the areas that were to be covered in ice to stop early heating. The straw was removed when the ice was crushed and sent down metal chutes to a crew waiting below. If the ice began to melt, the straw was quickly placed over it to keep it cool.

Contestants landed on seven to eight inches of the particles on the landing hill, and as a way to slow them down, hay and straw were spread at the bottom. A huge pile of hay was placed at the end of the out-run in case a jumper could not stop. Many a jumper ended up taking a dive into that pile.

The first summer competition brought in thousands of spectators, who could enjoy a jumping competition without having to stand in frigid temperatures. Top jumpers flocked to the forty-meter jump and found its fast landing surface a new challenge. Among the entries were Laurent Bernier from Quebec, the Dions, Charlie Tremblay of Dartmouth, Ken Fysh from Berlin and local jumpers Jimmie Darling of Laconia and John Veazey.

Laurent Bernier of Quebec, Canada, easily won class A. Eugene Levasseur, a twenty-year-old groundskeeper from the Scandinavian Club in

A jumper waits his turn to take flight from the forty-meter jump during a summer ski jumping competition. *Courtesy of Bob Bolduc.*

Worcester, outclassed the field of competitors by a wide margin and took home the Class B trophy. He became the man to beat.

At the end of 1949, a new trail named Tiger was opened next to Phelps. However, conditions at the Area had reached their lowest point. John Proctor had left the previous year in order to pursue his dream of owning and operating Proctor's Pine Tree Lodge in Laconia. Commissioner Norman Hubbard stepped in as an interim manager until Herbert "Red" Hayner assumed the position. This left the commissioner more time to actively seek out the next manager of the recreation area.

During the December meeting of the chamber of commerce, a large number of local residents showed up to protest the deplorable conditions at their recreation area. Arthur Nighswander showed photographs he had taken of the conditions. Henry Witt of King's Grant Inn, Fred Nachbaur of the Arlberg Inn and Bill Stockwell of the Baraks were among those present who urged long-term planning for the future of the Area. The Belknap Mountain Red Cross Ski Patrol joined in the protest and wrote a letter to the county commissioners protesting the condition of the trails and slopes. The amount of brush on the trails was creating a definite safety hazard. Fred Nachbaur was so concerned about the conditions that he installed his own lift on the slope located at the Arlberg Inn.

The single chairlift was shut down in January 1950 and was ordered to stay idle until April. Insurance was cancelled after the lift was deemed unsafe because the cable needed to be replaced. The minimum work required to be done at the Area consisted of tramway repairs and road resurfacing estimated at close to $50,000, with about half of that needed to restore the chairlift.

Commissioner Hubbard continued to actively look for the next manager and knew that it was going to take just the right individual to pull the recreation area out of its postwar slump. He had someone in mind and had been busy trying to convince that man to accept the position. Everyone knew the Area was teetering on the brink of disaster. The massive investment that had been made was about to be lost.

FRITZIE BAER

The Man in the Red Hat

From the time I was born until I was eight years old, I thought my grandfather "owned" a ski area. On many winter days, I was awakened early to drive out to the Area with Grampa Baer. With his bright red hat and constant cigar, he was larger than life to this little boy as we rode in the SnoCat while he groomed the slopes early on those mornings. Those are still very warm and happy memories from my childhood.

–Bob Arnold, grandson of Fritzie Baer

Frank "Fritzie" Baer made his first appearance in the Lakes Region by roaring into the area with a large number of motorcycles and their riders following closely behind. They were there for the challenging two-hundred-mile national championship race scheduled to be held in 1938 at the new recreation area located in Gilford.

Each year, the crowds attending the motorcycle event in June grew. Baer quickly gained a reputation as being a highly skilled and talented promoter. He also became known for rarely being seen without his infamous red hat and cigar. Entranced, the press began to report his every move.

Reporters found great interest in the announcement made at the beginning of April 1950 that Fritzie had been convinced by Commissioner Norman Hubbard to become manager of the Belknap Mountains Recreation Area. He reportedly refused two lucrative promotional positions on the West Coast due to his love of the Lakes Region and happily signed a two-year contract with the county commissioners. Shortly before he was hired, the commissioners appointed an advisory committee and instructed the members to outline the most important tasks required to bring the Area into a competitive state, keeping in mind the financial limitations.

More of a motorcycle man than one who had experience in the ski business, Fritzie had his work cut out for him at his new occupation. However, he knew how to promote, had connections and knew how to motivate people. Immediately, he began promoting the Area as a year-round recreation spot, calling it the prettiest spot anywhere in the country. He proceeded to put out a call to all clubs to use the recreation area for their activities since it was, in reality, something belonging to them. Almost immediately, positive change began to take place, and summer activities were being scheduled at a blistering rate.

His philosophy of promotion included the belief that in order to promote something, it had to be of the highest quality.[28] In the days before snowmaking, he insisted that grass and brush on ski trails be maintained at a very low height. Using only a bulldozer and elbow grease, Area employees manicured the slopes to a point that a car could be driven up and down them quite comfortably. This procedure opened the door for an earlier start to ski season. Now, with only a few inches of snow from Mother Nature, skiers could begin schussing their way down the mountain.

At the beginning of the ski season in 1950, the new and improved recreation area had become the main focus of the press, which reported on each upgrade. That summer, the ski meet on the forty-meter jump brought in hoards of newspaper, radio and television reporters, all eager to cover the event. The field of competitors was looking to beat Eugene Levasseur, but this year, in front of more than four thousand spectators, it was Ken Fysh's turn to shine as he won the Class A competition.

By March 1951, records were set for money receipts as well as for skier activity. Groups from all over New England were arriving in chartered buses and were greeted personally by the man in charge. Local inns and lodges were filled to capacity, and young people braved the cold weather and slept in sleeping bags at various spots throughout the woods. Jammed parking lots gave birth to the idea for additional parking space, which was added that May.

While promoting winter sports, the popularity of motorcycle events at the Area continued to grow and helped increase the off-season revenue.

During the summer of 1951, before a scheduled renovation of the sixty-meter landing hill, motorcycles roared up the mountain during the National Hill Climb event. For the first time since its inception, the recreation area appeared to have come fully into its own.

The annual summer ski jumping competition in 1951 was an even greater spectacle than it had been in prior years. During this round of summer jumping, the father-son team of Ernie and Roger Dion took home the coveted trophies. Ernie won top honors in Class A, while his twelve-year-old son won the Class C meet. Local competitors included Bill Trudgeon and John Veazey of Laconia.

One of the most endearing events ever held at the Area was carefully planned and brought to fruition on March 21, 1952. Operation Snowball was organized to connect the schoolchildren of Laconia with the schoolchildren of San Juan, Puerto Rico. Two tons of snow, worth an estimated ten thousand snowballs, were packed into two huge insulated bags. Victor Bowen, principal of Laconia Junior High School, brought seventeen children to the recreation area to help pack snow into the bags. Unable to contain themselves, the children had a massive snowball fight before getting to work.

Once the containers were filled with snowballs, they were driven to Logan Airport in Boston, where their shipment was supervised by Lou Noland, chief of operations at the airport. The bags were then loaded into a special cargo carrier attached to the belly of an Eastern Air Lines Constellation.

Upon the arrival of the never-before-seen snow in San Juan, mayhem broke out. Tens of thousands of people, most of them children, poured into the Munoz Rivera Park. All of them wanted to become part of the very first snowball fight ever to break out anywhere on the island. They, like their counterparts up north, participated in a snowball fight that raged continuously for half an hour. Seeing how quickly snow melted in the heat, the children quickly built a snowman, and the mission had been accomplished.

By 1952, while the Area was bubbling over with winter activities, something else was beginning to simmer. Fritzie was finding that the politics of having to run the recreation area with three county commissioners constantly looking over his shoulder was becoming unpleasant. He was invited to speak before the Laconia Rotary, where he spoke highly of the Area but explained that he already decided he would not renew his contract, which was due to expire at the end of April. Offering an example to the group, he recalled that a meeting of the county delegation had to

Local schoolchildren pack snowballs for shipment to Puerto Rico for Operation Snowball. *Courtesy of Ray Reed.*

be called in order to meet payroll even though one of the most prosperous seasons was well underway.

While Fritzie was struggling with his mixed feelings, the same thing was happening with the county commissioners and local residents, who once again discussed an area authority plan. Proposals to turn the enterprise into a nonprofit organization or sell it entirely were explored. Many were uneasy about the fact that it was not known who would become responsible for a deficit, should it occur. Skiers were not deterred, however, and they continued to arrive in great numbers. They were filled with demands for longer, faster trails and shorter lift lines and were fully prepared to travel to any ski area that would provide them with what they wanted.

Just after New Year's Day 1953, the addition of a groomer, called the SnoCat, propelled Belknap into the modern age of snow grooming. The new workhorse arrived just in time to prepare the slopes for the biggest and busiest weekend ever experienced at the Area. The shop crew quickly made

Fritzie Baer at the controls of his beloved SnoCat, the first piece of snow grooming equipment used at the ski area. *Courtesy of Arnold/Baer Family Library.*

up a special disk-harrow attachment that could easily break up hard surfaces, further advancing the capabilities of the groomer.

Fritzie was not content to sit idle and rest on the ski area's laurels. During the next meeting of the county commissioners, he asked them to consider appropriating no more than $50,000 for the installation of a new T-bar lift running from the bottom of Viking to the top of Tiger.[29] His stated reason for this request was to bring the Area in line with other ski areas and make it competitive.

Members of the ski patrol were present during the meeting and reminded everyone present that there had already been two accidents on the rope tow servicing the trails. An extension had been added to the rope tow requiring skiers to switch ropes on the way up. All felt that a T-bar lift would be far safer. The commissioners, understanding the need for this lift and seeing the tremendous public support for it, quickly voted in favor.

During the summer, the Belknap County Legislative Delegation did not hesitate to have Fritzie sign a two-year contract since he had been without one since he signed the original paperwork in 1950. Tossing politics aside and with renewed energy, he and his second-in-command, Maynard Libby, set out to improve as much as was reasonable with a very limited budget. His only goal had been, and remained, to make Belknap the number one spot for skiing and recreation.

The summer and fall months were spent installing the new 2,300-foot lift and the construction of a new trail: Red Hat, named after that familiar milliner's creation worn by the manager. Built to give experts a run for their money, it was much steeper than the neighboring Tiger. The new lift was designed to service both trails. By the opening of the 1954–55 ski season, both the T-bar lift and the new trail were ready for skiers.

Meanwhile, the Winnipesauke Ski Club was hard at work at what it did best. Bill Trudgeon, always a Class B jumper, had moved up into Class A.

Bill Trudgeon carefully aims as he leaps from the sixty-meter through the Hoop of Fire. *Courtesy of Alison Thibodeau and Brian Trudgeon.*

Still a leader in the club, he was now one of its best ski jumpers. No one was better at continually coming up with new and exciting stunts to entertain the public, much to the delight of the Area's manager. One of his most amazing spectacles was the construction of a large metal hoop at the takeoff point of the sixty-meter jump. Club members then wrapped it with burlap and set the entire hoop on fire. To the astonishment of onlookers, Trudgeon became the first jumper to leap through the unforgettable Hoop of Fire.

The pace of the 1955 ski season was unrivaled by any season to date. Fritzie easily kept up with the quick-fire requests and opportunities presented to him. In January, a letter to the editor appeared in the *Laconia Evening Citizen*. The writer felt that children in Belknap County were charged far too much to go skiing. The commissioners immediately voted to reduce the rates for any school-aged child in the county. Bus transportation from Laconia to the Area was arranged by the Kiwanis Club. A few days later, it was announced that skiing had become the latest addition to Laconia's Adult Education program. On Wednesday evenings, Phelps would be lit and available for those adults wishing to take lessons on the mountain.

By February 1955, skier visits were breaking all previous records. Each weekend, the number of skiers would break the attendance record of the previous weekend. One weekend during the month, eight buses arrived from the Liberty Mutual Insurance Company in Boston, along with two more buses from Boston. Cars packed the three parking lots to capacity.

The increasing attendance records paled in comparison to the smashing success of a teenage skier from Gilford named Penny Pitou. Learning to ski with the Gilford Outing Club and training on Fletcher Hale, she was quickly becoming an international skiing star. In March of that year, she was named as an alternate on the women's Olympic ski team. This fueled the popularity of downhill skiing and the ski area where she trained and raced. Watching this young woman take on the world of skiing was one of Fritzie's biggest thrills. He later was honored to have the opportunity to give her a lifetime pass to her hometown ski area.

The phenomenal ski season during 1955 gave the county commissioners every confidence that the Area was on track to becoming a consistent moneymaking enterprise. Fritzie told the commissioners that he predicted that the annual income of the Area in the next few years would be well into the six-figure range.

There were more highs than lows during the years Fritzie ran the Area, and his management skills were greatly tested during the lows. In June

1955, President Dwight Eisenhower paid a visit to the recreation spot as he toured the Lakes Region as part of a statewide tour. Six days later, during the annual motorcycle race, a Connecticut man was killed when he and two additional riders were involved in a serious accident. This accident was a foreshadowing of what was to come the following summer.

One year later, in July 1956, an accident involving the chairlift occurred, killing one man and injuring seven others. The tragedy resulted in new regulations for the industry, but negative attention rained down on the recreation spot. Fritzie remained a steadfast and undaunted leader throughout; he always kept clearly focused on his goal and successfully weathered any negative publicity.

While management worked to get the lift back up and running, the Winnipesaukee Ski Club saw the result of a project members had been working on for a year. In September, it announced that the North American ski jumping and cross-country championship meet would be held at Belknap. It was the first time in its twenty-five-year history that the organization would hold the meet in the East. Laconia residents and ski club members Harold Wescott, John Veazey, Irving Buell, Mel Morance, Dick Persons and Jon Riisnaes were members of the jump committee seeking to have the meet held locally.

As part of a statewide tour, President Eisenhower paid a visit to the Belknap Mountains Recreation Area. *Courtesy of Ray Reed.*

John Veazey had been a highly involved member in this committee, and for a year before the announcement, he had worked tirelessly to improve the jumps and was instrumental in bringing a number of key championship meets to the local jump. He and committee members sought and gained $5,000 to improve all four jumps, which led to Belknap's largest jump being patterned after the Olympic hill in Cortina, Italy.[30] John would remain involved with the Area's activities throughout his life and became a respected businessman and politician.

Through all the ups and downs, the talented promoter at the helm of the Area never once failed to sing the praises of the entire Lakes Region and everything it had to offer. His promotional skills helped Annalee Thorndike of Meredith, who was an annual participant in the Area's summer craft show, expand her business. A display of her whimsical, elflike dolls dressed as skiers often accompanied Fritzie to Boston trade shows. In 1963, her famous ski dolls graced the cover of the *Northland* catalogue, and as the company expanded its variety of dolls, it grew to be an international corporation.

Throughout many decades, civic leader and local businessman John Veazey became an integral part of Gunstock's history. *Courtesy of Phyllis Veazey.*

World-renowned Annalee Dolls of Meredith, New Hampshire, were promoted at trade shows by Fritzie Baer. *Courtesy of Gunstock Area Commission.*

Because of his hard work at the Area and beyond, at the end of 1958 Fritzie was proud to report to the commissioners that the annual income of the area had reached $200,000.[31] Despite this fact, New Hampshire senator James Rogers had become vocal about the county seriously considering selling the recreation area, saying that the Area was "literally bursting at the seams, and needed a serious expansion, which the county could not fund."[32] Again, the subject of who should oversee its operations surfaced. County Commissioner Joe Smith proposed a five-member authority to direct the Area; Commissioner Norman Hubbard flatly opposed the idea.

Fritzie fully supported the idea of a five-member organization, even though he realized that it would most likely mean that he would have to retire from his position. Letting his bosses deal with their unrest, in January 1959 Fritzie and his advisory committee proposed the expansion of the ski area to include the development of the summit of Gunstock Mountain, which would require a new lift complex. He saw it as being the key element to improving the all-season operations of the Area. Many questioned whether the expansion was necessary and whether the proposed trail system would tie in with the present trails at the base of the mountain. Committee members looked over aerial photographs taken by Gilford photographer and artist Loran Percy to see if the expansion was feasible, but they stated a far more in-depth study would have to be done. Fritzie stood firm on his opinion that without the full development of Gunstock Mountain, skiers would head to other areas with longer, steeper trails and would be chased away by the long lift lines that they faced at Belknap.

Fritzie continued to be vocal about the commissioners not listening to his suggestions or providing him with the necessary funds to make badly needed improvements and repairs. At the January 1959 meeting of the Laconia Rotary, he once again spoke of his unsatisfactory dealings with the county commissioners, especially Commissioner Joseph Smith. Each time he made suggestions or asked for certain things, they were flatly refused. He further told the group that he had been moved to resign numerous times due to the strained relations and the uncooperative stance adopted by the entire commission. One month later, in February, a bill was drafted outlining the management of the Area by a five-member commission.

Among a whirlwind of politics and disagreements, both Fritzie and his son and assistant, Bobby, were dismissed on June 23, 1959. The only reason offered to him for his dismissal was that there had been much criticism of the recreation area's management. Defending his management, Fritzie said that the enterprise never took in much money before he came along; he had increased revenue and was always careful not to have it ever cost the taxpayers of the county any tax dollars.

The commissioners merely stated that they had discussed his dismissal months before when he had publicly criticized them. Local officials and members of the public hoped that the new five-member commission would rehire their beloved manager when it took over. His large number of admirers knew that the Lakes Region would not see anyone like him again.

Fritzie asked to be considered along with the other candidates for the position, but he was not rehired. He worked until July 10, when Commissioner Norman Hubbard began serving as acting manager. Maynard Libby was appointed foreman, replacing Bobby Baer. Oddly, the new Joe Smith Trail was dedicated on Fritzie's last day as manager, even though the trail would not be finished until the beginning of September. Fritzie was in attendance at the ceremony despite the fact that he and the commissioner had been at odds for quite some time. However, no one could deny the fact that Joe Smith had a lengthy list of contributions to winter sports in the Lakes Region and to the development of the recreation area.

On August 13, 1959, the Belknap County Legislative Delegation elected the five-member commission consisting of members Dana Beane Jr., Dr. A. John Lacaillade, Mrs. Mary Robertson, Whitman Ide and Dr. William Baker. Elections were made in a three-hour executive session of the delegation. The new Belknap County Recreational Area Commission would take on the responsibility of supervising the Area on September 15, 1959. They now had the task of finding a new manager who could guide the recreation spot into a completely different arena.

Motorcycle man Fritzie Baer will forever be remembered for his many contributions to the world of motorcycles. He remained involved in the motorcycle races at the Area until they came to an end in 1963. To honor his lifelong dedication to the world of motorcycles, he was inducted into the AMA Motorcycle Hall of Fame in 1998.

To the residents of the Lakes Region, he is known as the man who pulled the Belknap Mountains Recreation Area out of a potentially fatal slump and made it a profitable and modernized enterprise. He achieved his goal of turning what had been a failing enterprise into a top competitor in the ski industry.

Fritzie Baer had a great love of motorcycles and brought the Gypsy Tour to the Lakes Region in 1938. *Courtesy of Arnold/Baer Family Library.*

Former New Hampshire governor Hugh Gregg summed up the thoughts of many in a public statement read at the fireworks celebration held in Laconia honoring this great promoter: "Even fireworks will never be heard over your noise promoting the Lakes Region. VIVA RED HAT!"[33]

FIRST CHAIRLIFT IN THE EAST

Celebration and Tragedy

I remember there was considerable discussion about that chairlift. They needed to figure out how to redesign something designed to bring bananas down the mountains of South America to something that could bring skiers up a mountain.

—John Veazey, civic leader and Laconia businessman

What was fashioned after a banana loader was turned into the first chairlift in the East, having been constructed on Mount Rowe during 1937. One year earlier, a similar chairlift had been installed in Sun Valley, Idaho. The design for the Idaho lift was the brainchild of Union Pacific Railroad engineer Jim Curran. His design was highly recommended by Charles A. Proctor, who had been working closely as an advisor to W. Averell Harriman, developer of Sun Valley. Proctor was also an advisor to Ed Willey of the Hussey Manufacturing Company, and it is probable that when Proctor returned to the East, he brought the design details for the lift back with him.

Hussey acted as general contractor for the project and managed the construction of the 3,200-foot Mount Rowe single chairlift. The deadline for completion of the lift was scheduled for January 1938. The American Steel and Wire Company of Worcester, Massachusetts, worked side by side with Hussey on the design and installation. The lift boasted two massive bull wheels provided by American Steel and Wire; the smaller wheel weighed in at one and a half tons, while the other tipped the scales at three tons.[34] The

Belknap lift also became the first chairlift in the country to be graced with towers made from steel.

Hundreds of laborers worked double shifts to ensure that the lift would be completed by the deadline. Captain Edward Lydiard made arrangements for an official dedication of the Belknap chair tow by Governor Francis P. Murphy during Governor's Day events in 1938. In front of hundreds and wearing a fashionable raccoon coat, he dedicated the new chair tow on February 5, 1938, just before he became its first passenger. Guests of honor included Fred Coleman and Ed Willey, who became the second and third passengers, respectively. They were followed by members of the press, who eagerly reported facts such as the lift being able to haul two hundred persons per hour at the rate of four hundred feet per minute.[35]

The idea of sitting in a chair while being transported up a mountain in just over five minutes captivated both skiers and nonskiers alike. Never before had anything like this been experienced in the Lakes Region. Passengers were allowed to ride both up and down the mountain in all seasons, and many used the lift to reach the top of Mount Rowe just to take in the spectacular views. During blueberry season, berry pickers utilized this new contraption as a far easier and quicker way to gain access to their favorite alpine berry.

The lift had many names throughout its life—chair tow, deluxe chair line ski tow, chair tramway—before finally becoming known as simply "the single chair." The lift was an experiment in the works, and there were a few bugs that needed to be worked out, the most noticeable being a jar when the lift either stopped or started. Laconia Malleable Foundry was called on to design and manufacture a special casting in the hopes of eliminating the annoyance. There was an obvious slack in the cable, which caused passengers to nearly hit the ground when getting on the lift or in spots where the terrain was closer to the chair. It was also quite noisy when in motion. Despite all of its quirks, it remained a popular attraction, always with long lines of passengers waiting their turn for a ride.

In December 1939, the upper terminal building was badly damaged by a fire, putting it out of commission. The fire was first noticed by an employee in the administrative building at the base of the mountain. A crew of men ready to battle the blaze hiked for nearly three-quarters of an hour up the long and winding Try-Me Trail. Upon arrival, they found that the fire had caused extensive damage and that the structure was a complete loss. Damage was estimated at a few thousand dollars, but there was no delay in the repair of the terminal.

As the lift aged, problems began to appear. In January 1950, the chairlift was completely shut down after the liability insurance was cancelled because the cable was found to be unsafe. It was decided that while replacing the cable, most of the lift should be replaced. Modern chairs, sporting both footrests and safety bars, were installed along with new hangers and pulleys. The overhaul left the framework as the only remaining original part of the entire system.

The work was done by employees under the watchful eye of a supervisor who had been hired specifically for the job. The project, totaling $25,000, was scheduled to begin in early April, with the idea of having it fully functional by the beginning of May.[36] Modernizing the lift and offering passengers a smoother, quiet ride were two goals accomplished during the overhaul. The act of creating a quieter ride would later cause the entire country to view chairlifts far differently than it ever had before.

Wednesday, July 25, 1956, was a typical hot and sunny summer day. Manager Fritzie Baer was out mowing grass. His son, Bobby, had just ridden

Even with daily inspections, tragedy struck when the chairlift cable snapped, killing one man and injuring seven passengers. *Courtesy of Ray Reed.*

down on the chairlift, which was faithfully bringing summer tourists up and down the mountain. Shortly after 10:30 a.m., for no apparent reason, the lift stopped and the cable appeared to slacken. A witness at the bottom of the mountain said that he heard a loud noise and heard the splashing of water. Looking up, he saw the chairs of the lift fall to the ground, section by section, like dominoes. He soon discovered that the chairs at the bottom had fallen into a small pond located nearby. All chairs and passengers on the lift had been hurled to the ground.

The cable of the lift had snapped about one hundred feet from the summit station. The tranquility of a lazy summer day had suddenly been turned upside down. One man was killed instantly when he was thrown onto the rocks below him. The victim was thirty-seven-year-old William M. Kirby, a machinist from Salem, Massachusetts.

In a twist of fate, Dr. L.H. Prior of Buffalo, New York, was a passenger on the lift. He became an uninjured victim and immediately began helping other passengers. He quickly discovered that Mr. Kirby had been fatally injured and continued to work his way down the mountain. Seven passengers were hurt, none critically, including Kirby's thirteen-year-old stepson, Arthur Paquette. Three of the victims were treated and released from the hospital; four remained hospitalized for a brief time.

A very pregnant Adele O'Neill was standing at the base with her two younger children watching the rest of her family ride up the mountain. Upon witnessing the accident, she ran up the mountain to reach her husband and her two additional children. All three had been injured. After her frantic climb, she, too, required hospitalization.

Fritzie had just finished mowing and was notified that there had been an accident. Immediately, he shut down all lifts operating at the Area and demanded that each be inspected. He showed his leadership capabilities by remaining calm throughout, orchestrating the rescue and answering all questions from family members of the victims and the press openly and honestly. While he handled the press, rescuers brought the body of William Kirby over the broken cable to the access road at a point just above the forty-meter jump. Last rites were performed there by Reverend Joseph Vachon, pastor of Sacred Heart Church in Laconia.

The victim's wife had taken the trip up to the top of the mountain slightly ahead of her husband. She was unaware that he had been killed and was taken down to the base of the mountain, where she was told of her husband's death. She collapsed, was taken to the hospital and placed under sedation. Her fifteen-year-old daughter, Jeanne Paquette, stoically accompanied her younger brother to the hospital so that he could receive treatment.

The stunned manager kept what could have become complete chaos firmly under control. It had to have been one of the saddest days of his life, yet he worked throughout the day to ensure that the tragedy was handled with the utmost respect for those involved. By nightfall, he was emotionally spent and was seen by a doctor, who had planned on checking on him as a matter of course. A dose of sleeping pills was prescribed, which offered a little bit of rest before the day after arrived.

The next day brought news of what had happened to the steel strand cable, which had been purchased from the American Steel and Wire Company during the 1950 lift overhaul. Ed Willey of the Hussey Manufacturing Company had been called and was on the scene. Also there were engineers from American Steel and Wire, John Herr and Vernon Kelsey, accompanied by Belknap County solicitor Thomas Cheney. After making a thorough inspection, Willey recommended a general overhaul of the lift before it was reopened.

It was discovered that between six to nine strands of the heavy steel cable had been holding the entire weight of the chairs and that the broken strands were corroded. The break occurred at the point where the cable was attached to the chair. Two lengths from around the point of the break were ordered to be cut by Sheriff Rodney Crockett. The sections were then taken to the Massachusetts Institute of Technology for extensive testing.

Sheriff Rodney Crockett orders sections of cable around the break to be cut. *Courtesy of Ray Reed.*

Upon close inspection, it was discovered that the steel strand cable had corroded, creating a weak point. *Courtesy of Ray Reed.*

No fault was found due to the fact that management had not only made required inspections but had also exceeded the requirements by inspecting the lifts on a daily basis. The most important determination made was that the detection of the cable damage was made nearly impossible due to a rubber sleeve covering the cable at the location of the break. That sleeve was added to the lift in 1950 for the sole purpose of making the ride quieter.

The lift remained closed for the rest of the summer per the orders of the Belknap County Legislative Delegation. The executive board of the delegation met in a closed session in September. It demanded to have proof that the lift was safe or it would not run again, citing that the passengers would demand it. In the eyes of the public, the chairlift had now lost some of its innocence.

A new cable arrived in mid-September and was installed at the end of the month. A custom woven-steel cable almost an inch thick was specially manufactured by the Bethlehem Steel Corporation and installed by Robbins and White of Westbrook, Maine. Half of the chairs were undergoing a reconditioning process.

Despite the diligence of the area's management and the replacement of most of the lift just six years earlier, the unspeakable had still happened. The chairlift became the focus of many throughout the nation, and the accident brought plenty of unwanted and negative publicity to the recreation area. As tragic as this event was, it forced new regulations to be set in place for the entire industry, and a new level of safety was reached for passengers of all lifts.

As a result of the accident, the New Hampshire Passenger Tramway Safety Board was formed in October 1956. By law, the four members of the board were to represent rope tow operators, cable tramways, the public and the insurance industry. The new board would have the authority to supervise and control all ski tows, lifts and tramways, including the design, construction and general operations.

For the duration of its lifetime, the lift's operations went smoothly thereafter. It remained in use even as bigger, faster and far more impressive chairlifts were installed around it. It was removed in 1978, as it had by then become completely antiquated with lift passengers looking to reach mountain summits in record time. Some of the chairs were put on display in the Powder Keg Lounge in the Main Lodge (formerly the Recreation Building). The rest were sold for $100 each, and a number of local residents made the investment in this piece of history. Several chairs currently hang in the museum section of Piche's Ski and Sports Shop in Gilford. All that is left behind of the first chairlift in the East are some of its chairs and wonderful memories of its slow, stop-and-smell-the-roses ride to the summit of Mount Rowe.

THE GILFORD OUTING CLUB

A Forty-Six-Year Odyssey

This was a small group of families that forged a big-time effort in shaping and helping their children have about as good a childhood as you could wish…There is no way we can ever thank Gary Allen for the direction he gave us all, from the smallest tot to the fastest racer.

–Marty Hall, U.S. and Canadian Olympic coach

The Gilford Outing Club, although not part of Gunstock, had a great influence on the direction of skiing in the Lakes Region and at Gunstock. The development of Gilford's top skiers and coaches often began with the outing club; their athletes later headed for the trails of Gunstock and could be found training on Fletcher Hale or on the jumps. Some of its members became Olympians and U.S. Ski Hall of Fame inductees, and one in particular won America's very first Olympic medal in downhill skiing.

As the Belknap Mountains Recreation Area struggled with its identity after World War II, a group of dedicated and energetic parents led by Gary Allen, Marty Hall Sr. and Gus Pitou founded the Gilford Outing Club in 1946. The mission of the club was to provide year-round family activities that encouraged friendship and community traditions.

For nearly fifty years, the organization taught hundreds of children how to ski and unleashed a golden era of volunteerism in town that remains unmatched to this day. Parent-volunteers used teamwork to make the organization run like a well-oiled machine, and they considered their time with the club sacred.

The Gilford Outing Club began its forty-six-year life on a modest slope off Schoolhouse Hill Road in Gilford. The organization started with nothing but soon hitched up an old car motor to run a rope tow, and when the time came for a warming hut, Gus Pitou rolled up with his old outhouse. With numerous members possessing so many different skills, any need or desire of the club could easily be fulfilled. In the early days, the Hall, Keller, Pitou, Stamps, Simons and Snow families were some of the families who contributed hundreds of hours of their time developing the organization, and in the process their children all became expert skiers and racers. Gilford's Olympic medalist, Penny Pitou, learned to ski on the club's slopes, as did Olympian Dick Taylor and Olympic coach Marty Hall.

The focus of the organization began with the sport of skiing, because as Gary Allen once remarked, "It was right after the war and people were weary—they really just wanted to get out and ski. But the Gilford Outing Club was so much more than that, it was also about hiking and swim meets in the summer." It did not matter that cash was scarce in those days, members' ingenuity filled in for what money could not buy.

In another part of town, just down from Gilford Village on Route 11A, Francis Piche and his brothers were running a small ski area with a rope tow and warming hut. During the 1940s, every rope tow in town was constantly in use during ski season, and this tow was no exception. The shack housing the motor for the tow sat abutting Potter Hill Road, just down the street from where the Allen and Pitou families lived.

In 1950, the club moved its operation to this new and improved location. With good equipment and challenging trails to use, the organization and its new ski area flourished. The trails were all given names, the most memorable being Bone-Crusher, a name requiring no further explanation. Fathers took turns running the tow and were skilled coaches as well. Mothers worked in the warming hut at the base of the slopes serving up hearty doses of encouragement, hot chocolate and refreshments to young skiers who sat warming themselves by an antique wood stove. Even today, the smell of wool mittens hung to dry by that stove still lingers in the minds of former members and remains one of their fondest memories.

The club added a snow groomer to its list of assets during the 1970s. Volunteer Don Chesebrough could almost always be found at the controls of the groomer during the winter, as well as cooking up massive quantities of clam chowder and barbecue chicken for meals in the summer and fall. Members

Fathers enjoyed manning the upper tow shack, which housed the engine for the rope tow. *Courtesy of Thompson-Ames Historical Society.*

had also developed a complex system of cross-country trails labeled with either yellow, blue or red markers signifying the level of experience required for each individual trail. The trail system stretched across the land of several residents on Potter Hill and ran along the base of the western side of Mount Rowe.

By the 1980s, a shift in society was apparent, and there were fewer parents willing to volunteer their time. They preferred to send their children to Gunstock for ski lessons. The larger ski area was rapidly expanding and was drawing more and more skiers of all ages to its slopes. Liability insurance costs began to skyrocket, crippling smaller ski operators. In the late 1940s, insurance costs for the club were about $150 per year. By the time the club disbanded, the cost of insurance had reached almost $6,000 per year, and never once had it filed a claim during its entire history. The lack of volunteers and young skiers and the untethered cost of insurance eventually led to the demise of the Gilford Outing Club in 1992.

When the club closed its affairs completely the following fall, its cash assets totaled nearly $4,000. The club proposed the creation of a scholarship fund

Hundreds of Gilford's children learned to ski with the Gilford Outing Club while making memories that would last a lifetime. *Courtesy of Gunstock Area Commission.*

through the Gunstock Ski Club. The main source of these funds was the Gus Pitou Fund, which had been established to honor everything that Penny's father had contributed to the junior racers in Gilford. This allowed her to remain active in the development of junior skiing, as she was always mindful of the sacrifices made by her family that had helped create the success she had in the Winter Olympics.[37]

Today, some of the former ski slopes used by the Gilford Outing Club remain open as the town's sledding hill. The land and the buildings belonging to the club were owned by Gary Allen and his wife, Lucile, and the couple donated the entire property to the Town of Gilford in 1994. Each winter, more and more families use the sledding hill as a way to enjoy some outdoor time together—reflecting on a small part of what took place on those slopes decades ago.

GARY ALLEN

Coach, Mentor, Ski Icon

I really try to be like Gary, but I know that I can't be everything he was, so I take something here and something there of what he was about, and from there I try to the best that I can be.

–Bob Bolduc, creator of Bolduc Park in Laconia-Gilford

It was standing room only at the Gilford Community Church during a memorial service held for Gary Allen on October 9, 2007. He had passed away a few days earlier at the golden age of ninety. His entire life had been filled with tremendous humility, hard work and a long list of admirers. A wide variety of individuals arrived at the church, prepared to pay their respects to their humble hero, including Penny Pitou, Marty Hall, friends, former high school students and, of course, his extensive family. It was a challenge for anyone in attendance to encapsulate what Gary had meant to them and how he had touched each of their lives. It was also impossible to describe the influence he had on Gilford and its outing club, the sport of skiing and the history of Gunstock.

The following June, his family once again came together to tell the life story of their adored husband, brother, father, grandfather and great-grandfather. Daily afternoon showers filled the summer season, and it was symbolic that the sun now prevailed. It had been his signature style to always find a reason to add a little bit of sunshine to the lives of others, and this day was no different.

They met in the clubhouse at Bolduc Park, joined by Penny Pitou and Bob Bolduc, in a room with walls appropriately lined with skis and an aroma of ski wax hanging in the air. The park, which offers golfing and cross-country skiing, was a place where Gary spent hundreds of hours with Bob as they designed its cross-country trail system. Eight months had passed since he had died, and it remained just as difficult for his family to tell the entire story of his life without leaving out any of his accomplishments.

Thomas Gary Allen was born in Montclair, New Jersey, on April 1, 1917. Sadly, a few years later his mother passed away, and he was raised by his father, whom he adored. His father, himself a gifted athlete, instilled a love of sports in him and his brother at a very young age. Christmas vacations were spent in Lake Placid, New York, where there was an abundance of opportunities to watch ski jumping. Gary was a graceful athlete throughout his life, excelling in many sports, including skiing, ski jumping and hockey. His preteen and teenage years were spent on a ranch out west where he became an expert horseman and cowboy.

He went on to graduate from Dartmouth College and then proceeded to become a naval aviator, flying bombers during World War II. An accomplished pilot, he was responsible for the training of new pilots, handpicking the men who would fly with him. His brother, John, explained that it was the war that caused Gary to focus on the good in life rather than resent the horrors that he had experienced. The war taught him true patience and understanding of his fellow man and that life should always remain an adventure. A man with high principals, he set for himself his own rules of conduct. It was of great importance to him to be a good example of an American and to be a consistent, positive role model for the men he was leading.

Returning to civilian life after the war, he was employed as a pilot for Pan American Airlines. He returned home to Gilford after long airline flights to live his life with his first wife, Lucile, and their five children. They all became members of the Gilford Outing Club, and his involvement with hundreds of the area's youth made a tremendous impact on their young lives. He gave up flying in 1952, preferring to spend more time with his family rather than jetting off to some foreign land.

Employment in the Lakes Region was found at the Northland Ski Company in Laconia, and the Allens' barn soon was filled up with skis for the use of young skiers so they would never be restricted by the lack of equipment. He obtained two master's degrees, one from Plymouth

Bill Trudgeon and Gary Allen congratulate the top competitors, along with Mezzie Barber at far right. *Courtesy of Gunstock Area Commission.*

State College and another from the University of New Hampshire. After becoming a math and science teacher at Laconia High School, he easily earned the spot as one of the students' favorites. Gary knew that it was essential to tap into the potential of every child, and the sooner it was done, the better. Consistent encouragement and praise for a job well done were always parts of his curriculum.

Family friend Penny Pitou always remained grateful to have had him as a coach during her formative years. She credited her former coach and mentor with giving her a moment of a lifetime as he helped her earn a spot on the Olympic team in 1955 when she was just sixteen years old:

> *Gary had the most incredible coaching style. Sometimes I would finish skiing and feel that I had skied so horribly and that everything I did, I did wrong. But he would never focus on the mistakes I had made, just on what I did right. That had such a positive impact on me. My son is a coach now, and I encourage him to coach the very same way Gary did with me.*

His son, Tom, explained his father's positive influence on the area's youth by saying, "There were sports in all the seasons, whether it was fishing, baseball, skiing or hiking. He could coach his own kids as easily as the other kids—there was never any pressure. My father always seemed to be able to help people when they were at a pivotal point in their lives; so many times he unknowingly changed the course of their lives."

Another son, Chris, was a tremendous outdoorsman and longed to experience the wilderness of Alaska; subsequently the family moved there for a few years. The elder Allen didn't hesitate to jump into a new life in Alaska with the same enthusiasm he had put into his life in Gilford. He taught school, skied and coached in his adopted state just as he had in New Hampshire. It didn't matter where he lived; his tremendous energy and optimistic spirit were part of his personality.

Fortunately for the Lakes Region, the Allens returned to their home in Gilford. Gary worked closely with Bill Trudgeon and Phil Cherveny as they founded the Gunstock Nordic Association, an organization focused on training ski jumpers and cross-country skiers from a very young age. The

Founders of the Gunstock Nordic Association Gary Allen and Bill Trudgeon pause during the 1976 U.S. Eastern Nordic Championships. *Courtesy of Gunstock Area Commission.*

men firmly believed in the theory that the sport of ski jumping would have an abundance of top-level senior jumpers if the investment was made in the early training of junior jumpers.

Close friend Bob Bolduc said of the man he admired, "Gary was a visionary in the sport of skiing. It sometimes took the industry a good ten years to catch up with some of his ideas." That vision helped create the snowmaking system on the jump hills at Gunstock. The system was so impressive that he was later hired to oversee the permanent installation of the state-of-the-art snowmaking and grooming systems on the ski jumps at Lake Placid before the Winter Olympics were held there in 1980.

Gary witnessed the beginning and the bittersweet end of the Gilford Outing Club. He was, at that point, the owner of the land and buildings formerly used by the organization and felt strongly that they should be donated to the town. He and his wife gave the property to the Town of Gilford in 1994, the same year he was inducted into the U.S. Ski and Snowboard Hall of Fame. His wife passed away a few years later.

He did everything with a sense of grace, including giving up what he loved the most. His second wife, Sara, explained that even though he was very active and involved in the organizations dear to him, he was good at knowing when to hand over the reins to the next generation. He never put away his skis, however, and as his long and productive life drew to a close, he had his wife capture a picture of him on skis in his ninetieth year.

Humility was his strongest trait, and not once did he ever crave the limelight; in fact, he shied away from it. Ultimately, it was impossible for him to deny his great influence on the sport he loved so much, and whether he would admit it or not, he changed the course of history in Gilford, at Gunstock and in the lives of the individuals lucky enough to have known him.

PENNY PITOU

Gilford's Fearless and Determined Olympian

It was always fun to ski with Penny and to coach her—she enjoyed everything, all facets of skiing. She probably was the most enthusiastic skier with the most guts of any skier I have ever known—and probably as strong a female skier and as competitive as you could find.

–Gary Allen, Penny's coach and mentor

Life began for Gilford's Olympic medalist Penny Pitou on Long Island, New York, in October 1938. When she was three, her parents, Gus and Lee, and younger brother, Kip, moved to rural Center Harbor, New Hampshire. Her father was longing to farm, and both he and her mother had fallen in love with the beauty of the Lakes Region. They purchased land and built a house. It was in the backyard of that house that Penny first began to ski.

After facing the challenges of farming and deciding that they wanted to live in a more populated area, the family moved to Gilford in the spring of 1946. Their new house, with its big set of front stairs, was just down the road from the house of another future ski icon, Gary Allen, who had moved there the very same year.

Fate was hard at work. With the formation of the Gilford Outing Club, the pretty, blond-haired girl learned to ski under the tutelage of some of the best and most patient coaches. Her childhood was one of freedom, the kind that allows for the growth of both the imagination and the physical self. The long, cold days of skiing in the winter, long hikes through the mountains and farm work in the summer toned the muscles of the young athletes and future Olympians. Many winter days were spent skiing at the Area, and then a quick schuss down the backside of Mount Rowe brought the tired children home.

Born with an abundance of intelligence, physical strength, good humor and the personality of a true leader, Penny was always at the top of her class. Her experiences with the Gilford Outing Club helped form the attitude she possesses to this day: the idea that she could accomplish anything. She explained the greatness of the outing club during an interview, saying, "With the outing club there were no divisions between the sexes. I never got the idea that I couldn't do something because I was a girl—it was really just one big family and we were all equal." She would soon find out that this same equality did not exist in the rest of the world.

When she was a student at Laconia High School, she joined the boys' ski team. A few years before, at age thirteen, she had begun to make headlines after she won a jumping competition in 1952. The press couldn't help but notice the girl who was beating all the boys. She was already considered one of the area's top skiers, along with fellow Gilford Outing Club members Dick Taylor, Marty and Linda Hall, Mike Wallace and the Keller boys, David and Scott.

One of her favorite memories of her time on the team was when she played a joke on officials during a race at New Hampton School. Tucking her long blond hair up under her hat, she told her teammates to call her Tommy. This worked until a fall caused her hat to fly off, revealing the fact that she was most definitely a girl. Much dismayed were the boys who discovered that the skier they were competing against wasn't a boy at all.

Shortly after the incident, she was called to the principal's office at school and informed that girls could no longer be on the ski team. She was winning races and helping the team, but the problem appeared to be the fact that there was no chaperone for her on the bus. Angry at the injustice of it, her anger was turned into determination. Being told that competing against the boys was now out of the question, she felt compelled to beat every single girl she would ever race against. This became her motivation and goal for her skiing career.

If there was any pressure to succeed, it came from within and not from her family. Approaching races with a good attitude and an even better attitude if a race was lost, Penny learned how to become one of the best skiers in

John O'Brien and Holland Whitney present the New England Council's Silver Bowl to the family of Penny Pitou: Kip, Lee and Gus Pitou. *Courtesy of Gunstock Area Commission.*

the world. Always eager to know what mistakes had been made and having a strong desire to correct them made her one of the best. Her coach, friend and mentor, Gary Allen, had an approach to coaching that complemented Penny's style of learning. Her mother credited him with giving her daughter the fundamentals she needed and said that he was the first to see her potential and tap into it. He outlined a rigorous training schedule and had the ability to create a good foundation in the fundamentals of skiing.

At Gunstock, Penny took one formal ski lesson, her only, with Maynard Libby. The ski jumps at Gunstock were used often by the promising young skier and her friends, as she explained how Gary believed that downhill racers should know how to handle being in the air:

> *I used to jump the ten- and twenty-meter when I was on the boys' ski team at Laconia High School. We needed to be comfortable in the air, so we would head over to jump at Gunstock. We would jump in the evenings, and*

> *it was bitterly cold. My mother would drive me over, and before I got out of the car, she would ask me if this was something I really wanted to do, and I would say, "Oh, yeah!" as I ran from the car.*
>
> *Lights had been installed with a box to put a quarter in to turn the lights on. We'd drop in a quarter, run up and hope the lights didn't go off while we were in midair. A few times they did—now THAT'S flying blind! It was survival of the fittest.*

While she continued to win one meet after another, Frank Hurt, a member of the Laconia High ski team, had qualified for the 1954 National Junior Downhill Slalom Championship in Jackson Hole, Wyoming. He became the first skier from the region to compete in a national event of this kind.

In 1955, Penny herself became the Junior National Champion by winning the national girls' downhill, slalom and combined titles in Whitefish, Montana. A rousing welcome awaited the high school junior upon her return to the Lakes Region, where she was met at the Laconia Tavern by dignitaries, friends and classmates.

Her skiing career was skyrocketing as she was chosen to be an alternate on the 1956 Olympic ski team. She immediately became a favorite with the press, who described her as pretty, charming and unassuming. Reporters followed her to the Area during the summer of 1955, when she and her fellow Olympic teammates made an appearance at the ski jumping competition held there in July.

Before heading to the Olympics, she competed in Grindelwald, Switzerland, where she sprained her ankle during a fall. Undaunted and focused on being the best, the future Olympian went from there to Kitzbuhel and Bad Gastein, Austria, once again spraining an ankle. At the 1956 Winter Olympics, at the tender age of seventeen, she skied all three events: downhill, slalom and giant slalom in Cortina d'Ampezzo, Italy. Even though no medal was won, she remained optimistic, didn't dwell on her losses and always looked to the future. In a letter to her parents that appeared in the *Laconia Evening Citizen*, she wrote:

> *The downhill was today. I took it all right and really crouched over the bumpiest bumps you ever saw. I was going like mad and my legs were good. The last schuss was fine but all of a sudden I hit a transition and fell flat on my face 25 feet from the finish line and lost too much time. Very embarrassing. Oh, well, there are bigger and better days ahead.*

The 1956 Olympic ski team at Belknap's summer ski jumping competition held in July 1955. Gilford's Penny Pitou appears at bottom left. *Courtesy of Bob Bolduc.*

Everything is over for the girls. We skied our hardest. Some had good luck, others creamed themselves. We all learned a lot and will benefit from this wonderful experience. I hope you are not too disappointed in my showings. I still have the A.K. downhill to do and many other races over here.

I'm sorry the Olympic games are over. Wish I could run that downhill again.[38]

"Dynamite" is what the Associated Press called her in February 1956 after a first-place win in downhill and second in combined at St. Moritz, Switzerland. Still a senior in high school, there was one more race: the Arlberg-Kandahar in Austria, an exceptionally grueling and dangerous race. She finished third, once again spraining an ankle. One week before returning home, she won second in the Grand Prix at Chamonix. That year, she was honored with the Andrea Mead-Lawrence Award, becoming America's Junior Skier of the Year. Mead-Lawrence was the female skier whom Penny idolized, and she credits her with giving her the proper motivation during the most critical times of her career.

Penny was back in the Lakes Region by the end of March, after spending three and a half months competing in Europe. She had competed in the Olympic games and six other major skiing events and her success was beginning to force a change in the world of skiing. After the impressive wins of this powerful female skier, Europeans for the first time had no choice but to take an American downhill skier seriously.

However, Penny wasn't thinking too far ahead; she was still a teenager and only wanted to get back to school, finish her schoolwork and graduate. Ranked fifth in her graduating class at Laconia High School; she continued on to Middlebury College, and her name was found on the dean's list during her freshmen year.

In a race in Grindelwald, Switzerland, held before the 1958 Alpine World Championships, she was hailed as a heroine by getting to her feet after a violent fall that caused a loss of almost ten seconds. Unstoppable, she finished the race covered head to toe with snow and still had an impressive finish. In competitions that followed in Austria, Italy and Poland, she never placed lower than second, placing first in downhill in the Coppa Femina in Abetone, Italy.

Every aspect of her young life seemed to be moving in fast motion, including what was appearing in newspapers and magazines. She asked her parents if they saw the interesting photo that appeared in *Life* magazine just as the competitive season was ending, writing in a letter, "How did you like me kissing the Russian in *Life*? It was in all the magazines over here, too. Crazy!"[39] The skiing star had no problem handling the press with a style and grace that reached well beyond her years.

Penny and fellow top American skier Betsy Snite were now world championship team members and were bound for eastern Europe after the ski season was over. She was unsure of what to do at this point in her life, but her parents advised her to take advantage of the travel opportunities. She remained in Europe, got a job at the Kastle Ski Factory and learned to speak German and French fluently.

In January 1959, the pair swept three of the four titles during the Grindelwald International Ski Meet. Penny was first in downhill and combined; Betsy came in second in downhill. After her wins, Gilford's sweetheart stepped firmly into the position of being the nation's main hope for a medal during the 1960 Winter Olympics. Both girls were ready for one more try for the gold, as Penny told reporters, "I am going to have a good try in Squaw Valley and then take my racing skis off for good, you know, I'm getting old."[40] She was just twenty years old.

Upon arriving home after being away for a year and three months, the skier-celebrity received personal congratulations from President Eisenhower and New Hampshire governor Wesley Powell, who had declared February 25, 1959, Penny Pitou Day. Overwhelmed by the welcome, she told the crowd that greeted her, "I'm very, very happy. But really, I'm not very much. I've only been trying to do my best."[41] Speaking to the legislature, she addressed

Penny is helped by her father, Gus, upon her arrival at the New Hampshire Statehouse during Penny Pitou Day. *Courtesy of Bob Bolduc.*

the captivated audience, which included a group of schoolchildren. After having seen some of the deplorable conditions in Europe, she told the children to appreciate what they have and what their parents did for them.

At the 1960 Winter Olympics, the intense pressure placed on this focused young woman was easily taken in stride. Penny Pitou made history by becoming the first American ever to win a medal in downhill in the Olympics, flying across the finish line one second behind the winner, Heidi Biebl of Germany. She captured another silver medal in giant slalom, one tenth of a second behind Yvonne Ruegg of Switzerland.

Following her huge win at the Olympics, she was inducted into the National Ski Hall of Fame in 1961 and was named Best Alpine Skier of the Year. By then, Penny, along with Egon Zimmermann, had returned home to Gilford. They caused quite a stir in the Lakes Region when the two top skiers signed on as directors of the Penny Pitou Ski School at the Area. The

Olympians Penny Pitou and Egon Zimmermann ran the successful and popular Penny Pitou Ski School located at Gunstock. *Courtesy of Gunstock Area Commission.*

stunning couple was married in February 1961 at the family home in Gilford with immediate family and a few neighbors present.

Penny's new husband was described as one of the best technicians in the sport and one of the top skiers in the world. A native of Innsbruck, Austria, he first started to ski and compete at the age of four, winning international races at eight. As a young teenager, he was already jumping off the eighty-meter jump in his hometown. At age sixteen, he was named to the Austrian National Junior Team and went on to win his country's Junior Championship in 1950. In 1958, he was named a member of the Austrian World Championship Team. He also became one of the most sought-after instructors.

The ski school hired only the best instructors, namely Norm Paquette and Willie Klein, an Austrian. Locals Fred Nachbaur and Maynard Libby also joined the team. Later, Klaus Buttinger and Pepi Herrmann came on board. During its first year, the school proved to be extremely popular, and the recreation area saw a better than 50 percent increase in business. It welcomed all types of skiers and ran lessons such as the well-attended Housewife Ski Course, for which more than fifty women would show up for their lessons in zero-degree weather. A second school was opened in 1963 at Blue Hills in Massachusetts as Penny and Egon became certified professional ski instructors.

The couple welcomed their first son, Christian, into the world in 1962. Three years later, their second son, Kim, was born. Not surprisingly, the boys learned to ski at the Area, skiing by the side of their famous parents and became accomplished skiers in their own right. A few years later, in 1968, Penny and Egon divorced. Egon stayed on with the ski school, and Penny was hired as a ski fashion consultant for White Stag. Her athletic accomplishments continued when she became one of the best female tennis players in New Hampshire. In the early 1970s, she coached a highly successful girls' ski team at Laconia High School.

In 1974, she bought the Lakes Travel Agency in Laconia and immediately changed its name to Penny Pitou Travel, Inc. Two additional branches were opened, one in Concord, New Hampshire, in 1979, and a second in North Conway in 1995. For more than thirty years, she has hosted skiing and hiking trips to the Alps, the same mountains she trained and raced on in her younger days.

The community she embraced as her own has fully embraced her back, and the skiing star will always remain a treasured resident of Gilford. Her

Above: Penny Pitou and Egon Zimmermann teach their son, Christian, how to "Ski Gunstock." *Courtesy of Gunstock Area Commission.*

Left: Penny Pitou, Gilford's two-time Olympic Silver Medalist, trained with the Gilford Outing Club and at the Belknap Mountains Recreation Area. *Courtesy of Gunstock Area Commission.*

résumé includes a long list of philanthropic pursuits, board affiliations and accomplishments both inside and outside the world of skiing. Even today, Penny is often thanked by women who know that she was one of the first to make the world acknowledge the abilities and potential of female skiers. Now a grandmother of three, she knows that because of her accomplishments and determined attitude toward life, doors were opened that had previously been shut tight, making the world a far better place in which to live.

FROM BELKNAP TO GUNSTOCK

Changes for the Area

The Lakes Region had everything my father wanted: the lakes and the mountains. That's what brought him here and that's what kept him here.
—Alison Thibodeau, daughter of veteran ski jumper Bill Trudgeon

Just before Penny Pitou headed to Squaw Valley to compete in the Olympics, the new Belknap County Recreational Area Commission's first task was to find a replacement for the ever-popular Fritzie Baer. With the advancement of technology regarding lifts, ski equipment and grooming, the popularity of downhill skiing soared, and the commission was looking for a manager who knew how to focus on expanding the Area and making it competitive. That manager was Warren Warner, who was named to the position in November 1959. A native of Shaftsbury, Vermont, he had extensive experience in the construction and development of ski areas throughout that state.

The major expansion of the ski area during the 1960s was fueled by the demands of skiers and the fact that Olympians Penny Pitou and Egon Zimmermann were now running the ski school. Residents and visitors alike were sold on the beauty and scenery of the Lakes Region; however, one of the biggest complaints heard about the ski area was that the trails were simply too short. Repeatedly, the eyes of management fell longingly to the high summit of Gunstock Mountain.

Dr. A. John Lacaillade, chairman of the new commission, announced that his group would push for a loan to pay for the complete development of

Gunstock Mountain before the development of the entire mountain. *Left to right*: Smith, Phelps, Viking, Tiger and Red Hat Trails. *Courtesy of Gunstock Area Commission.*

Gunstock Mountain. With a loan in hand, three hundred additional acres that encompassed the summit were purchased. The Area's name, Belknap Mountains Recreation Area, no longer seemed to fit the mission of the facility. In order to advertise the upcoming expansion, the Area was called Gunstock for short, and an official name change to Gunstock Recreation Area occurred shortly afterward. In keeping with its new name, additional trails from that point forward were given names related to firearms.

The move away from skiing on Mount Rowe was set into motion. The slalom course, Fletcher Hale, although an impressive racecourse, was eventually abandoned in the late 1970s mainly because it had always been a challenge to groom. Slalom races were brought over to Red Hat. The sixty-meter jump went into a period of dormancy, although Bill Trudgeon and Gary Allen kept a large number of junior jumpers soaring from the ten- and twenty-meter jumps.

An aggressive transformation was in the works; it began with the installation of a Doppelmayr T-bar lift on the brand-new Joe Smith Trail, and later an additional trail, Cannonball, was cut between Tiger and Red Hat. The goal was to have all race competitions held on the Cannonball Trail.

In 1962, four new trails reaching to the summit of Gunstock Mountain were added. Perched at the top overlooking the entire facility, a warming hut called the Panorama Pub was constructed, and more night lighting was installed. A new double chairlift was constructed to the summit, and once completed it became the longest in the state. The lift was installed by Werner Wagner, a native of Switzerland and an employee of Mueller Lifts. By 1964, he had settled in Gilford, owned his own tramway service company and installed the second double chairlift to the summit. The two side-by-side double chairlifts became known as the Double Double.

Two more lifts were added during the massive expansion. In 1966, yet another Doppelmayr T-bar lift was installed on Tiger Trail and became the only illuminated T-bar in New England. It serviced three trails: Stone Bar, Tiger and Red Hat. In 1969, a T-bar was constructed on Phelps, bringing the number of T-bar lifts in use to three.

Later in the decade, a new general plan for Gunstock was presented to the commission, and for the first time a request for the installation of

Gunstock Recreation Area following the development of Gunstock Mountain and its summit. *Courtesy of Gunstock Area Commission.*

snowmaking equipment was included. Also requested were more lifts and the repair of all four ski jumps. The proposals clearly were the result of the demands of skiers and year-round recreationalists. An abundance of beautiful scenery and spectacular views had become secondary for Gunstock; it constantly battled the lack of elevation, which for the northern ski areas was a nonexistent problem.

Dave Buckman arrived at Gunstock in 1971 as its new public relations director. A talented photographer, he captured some of the most striking images of Gunstock on record. These images appeared in newspapers throughout the region to promote the advantages of the year-round playground in the Lakes Region. Shortly after he arrived, he had something brand new to photograph.

It was in 1971 that artificial snow made its debut at the bigger and better recreation area. During the first week of February, the snowmaking system designed by Jeff White, president of North American Engineering Corporation and designer of SNOTROL, was officially tested at Gunstock. The sixty-acre system took three months to build, and once completed, it became the state's largest snowmaking system. Snow could now fall on

Waiting for Mother Nature to provide snow became a thing of the past when snowmaking arrived at Gunstock. *Courtesy of Gunstock Area Commission.*

certain trails at the rate of almost one foot per hour, all being directed through a huge compressor building now standing at the base of the mountain. Warren Warner called it the most advanced snowmaking system in the industry, requiring little maintenance and low personnel input.

Early in the 1970s, the commissioners outlined numerous major projects, including the addition of another base lodge called the Stockade Lodge and the creation of the Pistol Complex with its own 2,300-foot chairlift and four trails. Three of the new trails were to be for intermediate skiers; one would be for novice skiers.

Werner Wagner was once again brought in for the installation of the double chairlift for the new Pistol Complex. This time, however, instead of hauling buckets of cement to the summit via a chairlift, the installation was much easier and faster. A helicopter was used to place lift towers. Once the lift and trails in the complex were complete, the ski area now had the most uphill cable, and Gunstock moved into the number one position. It

Towers for the new Pistol lift were swiftly and skillfully placed by helicopter. *Courtesy of Gunstock Area Commission.*

had grown from being known as a local recreation area to one that had prominence both on the regional and national levels.

As the decade wore on, Warren Warner was replaced by Ernest Hegi in 1975, and the ski school continued on without Penny Pitou. Egon Zimmermann stayed on as director of the Gunstock Ski School and had gained a worldwide reputation for his excellence as a ski instructor. He offered his popular Graduated Length Method of learning, a five-day learn-to-ski package promising that new skiers would be skiing linked parallel turns with polish by the end of the course. Still in use for those beginning students was a rope tow on the beginner's trail, Kitty Kat. The tow stood as a symbol of Gunstock's past but would not survive further expansions.

As always, Gunstock's influence continued to spill out into the local community. The development of what would become New Hampshire's largest subdivision began in the late 1960s with the promotion of Gunstock Acres, a community filled with houses built in the style of Swiss ski chalets.

A symbol of Gunstock's past, a rope tow on the beginner's trail, Kitty Kat, was in use during the 1970s. *Courtesy of Gunstock Area Commission.*

Marketed by the Boston real estate firm American Heritage Properties, it included in its list of assets the all-season Gunstock Recreation Area.

The old ski lodge, the Baraks, went through a transformation of its own, including a short stint as elderly housing. It then became the clubhouse for the brand-new Gunstock Acres and experienced upgrades and expansions of its own, including the addition of an Olympic-size skating rink, a toboggan run, a riding ring, tennis, handball and basketball courts, as well as a beginner's ski slope.

The community soon faltered after experiencing financial difficulties. The clubhouse was sold to private owners, and the residents, mostly seasonal, no longer had access to its facilities. It changed hands several times, went through another round of major renovations during the 1980s and is today known as the Gunstock Inn and Fitness Center. Throughout all its changes, some of the original, historic beams from the Baraks have remained and are part of the décor, along with a photo gallery showcasing the ski history of the inn.

Once known as the Baraks, the former ski lodge became a clubhouse for the state's largest subdivision, Gunstock Acres. *Courtesy of Ray Reed.*

Another local establishment, the Arlberg Inn, was sold by the Nachbaur family in 1973 and did not retain its status as a favorite gathering place for skiers and members of the community. Francis Piche sold his ski equipment business to his longtime assistant, Bob Bolduc. Bob further expanded Piche's Ski and Sports Shop, keeping the store in Gilford and adding another location in Belmont, New Hampshire. Over the years, the business has remained a leading competitor in the industry and is considered a landmark in the Lakes Region. With a history as long as that of Gunstock, it has fit generations of skiers with high-quality equipment.

The expansions of Gunstock during the 1960s and 1970s were just the beginning of many more that followed. However, the expansions taking place during these decades kept the facility financially independent from the taxpayers of Belknap County. The management and operation of the recreation area had finally been ironed out, but one longtime question remained unanswered: what would happen should a deficit occur?

GUNSTOCK NORDIC ASSOCIATION AND GUNSTOCK SKI CLUB

One Shall Become Two

Gary felt so strongly that there had to be an active program for the young kids, that you had to start kids when they were young or they would find some other program to get involved with and you'd lose them.
–Sara Allen, wife of the late ski icon Gary Allen

Dad always used to say, "Once you take that leap, for a few brief seconds, you know what it's like to soar like a bird."
–Brian Trudgeon, son of ski jumper and coach Bill Trudgeon

Throughout all of the changes that occurred at Gunstock, the Winnipesaukee Ski Club had always stood as a strong anchor on the local and regional level. The club went through as many changes as the ski area, and now, Gunstock had become a completely new entity with a new focus. Those changes rippled through the ski club, and the two disciplines of skiing, Alpine and Nordic, evolved into separate organizations.

Nordic sports at Gunstock were struggling due to the extreme interest in downhill skiing and the extensive development of Gunstock Mountain. Gary Allen and Bill Trudgeon, two men who had already made their mark in the sport, continued to work with junior jumpers.

In 1969, they, along with Phil Cerveny, founded the Gunstock Nordic Federation and focused on junior jumpers. One year later, the Gunstock Nordic Association was founded for the benefit of older juniors and senior

With the formation of the Gunstock Nordic Association, the Lakes Region's tradition of hosting national and international jumping competitions returned. *Courtesy of Gunstock Area Commission.*

Nordic competitors. In 1972, the two organizations merged, keeping the name of Gunstock Nordic Association.

While coaching ski jumpers and cross-country skiers, the men focused on rebuilding all four jumps at Gunstock. Up-to-date European hill profiles were obtained, and lights were installed on all hills except at the sixty-meter jump. The judges' building was reconstructed, as the original building had burned down a number of years before. One by one, the jumps became usable, and the number of members in the organization mushroomed.

The association was experiencing tremendous growth partly because of the philosophy that it was the younger children who made a program successful. Gary Allen explained the importance of focusing on the junior members during an interview in 1994:

> *I was always interested in the little kids and the juniors…even back in the '60s with Bill Trudgeon—we always had lots of little kids in our program. To me that is what is important. If you don't have little kids*

> *coming along, then pretty soon you don't have any program at all. So, that's been my interest—from beginning to end—developing the juniors. The seniors will take care of themselves.*[42]

Junior members were not experienced enough to take flight from the sixty-meter jump, but the jump received the most attention and renovation work in 1976 when it was turned into an Olympic-caliber, seventy-meter jump. The rotted start house that had looked down on almost forty years of jumping history was removed and never replaced. A steel extension was added, giving the jump more length and height. After renovations were complete, it received one of the earliest FIS hill certifications in this country.[43] The change in the size of the jump also resulted in the retirement of Torger Tokle's record made on the sixty-meter jump.

The sport of ski jumping at Gunstock was experiencing a rebirth, and by 1975, it saw the most activity, with forty-five junior jumpers and eighty-two cross-country skiers. The organization hosted the USSA Nordic Combined

The removal of the sixty-meter jump start house took place before the jump was transformed into an Olympic-size seventy-meter. *Courtesy of Gunstock Area Commission.*

Championships, the National Jumping Championships, the Gunstock International FIS and the National Nordic Combined Championships. Roger Holden of Norway came along and set the new hill record on the seventy-meter with a leap of 253 feet.

The association produced numerous high-level Nordic athletes. Teyck Weed competed in the 1972 Olympics, Glen Joyce became a member of the U.S. national team and Kurt and Chase Kling competed in the Junior National Championships. Our country's Junior Olympics saw thirteen of the association's members compete during the 1980s. Two of the most notable Nordic combined athletes from the organization were Jim and Chris Leggett, who both have outstanding records at the junior and senior level.

Talented athletes found great benefit from the coaches and mentors they found with the Gunstock Nordic Association. However, snowmaking had not been installed at the jumps, and the lack of snow continued to be a problem for training and competitions. In 1976, Gary Allen made his first attempt at snowmaking on the seventy-meter jump. The next year, he was hard at work developing a hefty roller with a winch and cable system for grooming and packing the landing hill. Two years later, snowmaking on the seventy-meter was completely successful, using portable snow guns from the snowmaking department at the ski area.

In 1980, the FIS International was held at Gunstock, and it easily became its most successful meet. The top jumpers in the world soared from the seventy-meter before heading over to the 1980 Winter Olympics held in Lake Placid, New York. In a return to the old days of ski jumping, more than six thousand spectators watched the competition along with the governor of New Hampshire and a host of celebrities. Bill Trudgeon then headed to the Olympics to become chief assistant to chief of hill. Gary was already in Lake Placid installing the snowmaking and grooming equipment on the hills.

The snowmaking system back at Gunstock continued to be perfected with the help of some older junior members, especially Chris and Jim Leggett. In 1986, temporary snowmaking became a thing of the past with a permanent system servicing all four jumps, and at the time it was one of the most complete ski jump snowmaking systems in the country.

The Gunstock Nordic Association can claim yet another noteworthy accomplishment of one of its members. Parent-volunteer Cynthia Kling, the mother of four Nordic competitors, donated endless hours of her time as a local, regional and national ski jumping judge. When she applied to

Gary Allen was instrumental in the development of snowmaking for the ski area's four jumps. *Courtesy of Gunstock Area Commission.*

become an FIS jumping judge, officials weren't quite sure what to do with a female applicant since no woman had ever applied. The application process took several years, but she successfully became the world's first and only female FIS jumping judge, chalking up another first for the organization.

The association today remains a successful group with a focus on cross-country skiing. A new system of trails was constructed at Gunstock, which attracts some of the top competitors in the Northeast. In keeping with its legacy, the organization is once again hosting some of the most important cross-country competitions in the region.

With the formation of the Gunstock Nordic Association, the Winnipesaukee Ski Club was no longer involved with Nordic skiing and began to focus on downhill skiing and junior racing. Members working on the reorganization of the club were highly ambitious individuals who wanted the club's focus to be on the development of junior racers.

In the late '50s, the club members made it their goal to teach every Laconia youngster how to ski. Returning to its roots, when the club jumped from a ski jump on Academy Street in Laconia, it set up a gentle slope there on acreage donated for the purpose of coaching junior skiers. The Public

Hundreds of junior racers have received top-notch training from the coaches of the Gunstock Ski Club. *Courtesy of Gunstock Area Commission.*

Works Department worked with club members to install lights so that lessons could be given in the evenings after school.

Large numbers of Laconia's children were given skiing lessons twice a week in the early evening. The club ran the ski area for a few years, and during those years, thousands earned their achievement bars. When Penny Pitou and Egon Zimmermann returned after the Olympics to run the ski school at Gunstock, Egon and the instructors were hired to give lessons at the Academy Street location. More and more the club was moving toward a race-oriented program, and weekend lessons at Gunstock eventually replaced the lessons given in Laconia.

Membership numbers were low, and a bumpy transition was made into the formation of a junior racer organization. The 1970s brought quick growth, and the club began doing business as the Gunstock Ski Club. It was reaching new heights but was failing to raise enough money to fund its ambitious goals. As a result, members began to rely almost

Gunstock Ski Club hosts numerous junior competitions each year, including races honoring Gus Pitou, Tony Buttinger and Francis Piche. *Courtesy of Gunstock Area Commission.*

entirely on the management of Gunstock, both for financial assistance and leadership skills.

It was the attitude of the times that Gunstock was required to support the youth in Belknap County. The ski area contributed more and more money to the club—paying all but 20 percent of its budget—had club coaches on Gunstock's payroll and purchased the necessary equipment. The club and its funding became a line item in the budget of the ski area. Both parties realized that this approach to the club's funding was unfortunate and inappropriate. The leadership of the club educated itself on how to manage a blossoming racer organization, and little by little, it gained complete financial independence.

Today, it does not rely on Gunstock for any funding, and the two organizations continue to work together in a cooperative manner. Club president Ruth McLaughlin is head of a well-run, parent-managed ski club that provides training and coaching for its 126 athletes and racers. Nearly seventy families actively participate in the running and management of its activities, and a few families retain their membership just for the social aspect of the organization.[44] Members built a warm and inviting clubhouse, which sits at the base of Gunstock's Cannonball racecourse.

The Gunstock Ski Club has a history extending far beyond that of Gunstock and has been at the core of the growth of skiing throughout the history of the sport in the Lakes Region. Its members have skied on all of the competitive trails in Gilford, beginning with the trails that the club created in the Belknap Mountains in the 1930s. No other ski club at Gunstock will ever be able to boast such a long and impressive history as the Gunstock Ski Club, nor will any have been fortunate enough to have had members who have skied through every decade of the recreation area's history.

THE CONTINUING EVOLUTION

Maintaining the Competitive Edge

Gunstock has remained on the cutting edge of family fun for seventy-five years, all the while maintaining a historic and rustic atmosphere steeped in tradition. We take our stewardship of this magnificent facility very seriously, and we are committed to our mission of providing fun and building traditions for generations of guests.
—Greg Goddard, general manager, Gunstock Mountain Resort

While the ski clubs at Gunstock were evolving and producing top athletes, Gunstock's evolution continued at a rapid pace. During the 1980 Winter Olympics, Heidi Pruess of nearby Lakeport placed fourth in the women's downhill event. Her win fueled a renewed interest in junior racing with the Gunstock Ski Club and downhill skiing at Gunstock.

During 1980, Dick Tapply was just stepping into his new position as general manager of the recreation area. Early in his tenure, Gunstock's largest expansion was outlined and brought to fruition. To remain competitive, about $10 million was spent on new lifts, trails and buildings and an expanded snowmaking operation.

Construction crews went to work with a vengeance, blasting away ledge and cutting new trails into areas filled with rocks. Nearly two dozen miles of snowmaking pipes were installed. A reservoir with a capacity of 80 million gallons of water was created to allow a reserve to be stored for the much larger snowmaking system.

In 1987, a walkway and deck were added between the Main Lodge and the Guest Services Lodge. *Courtesy of Gunstock Area Commission.*

In 1986, three new lifts were added: the Ramrod Quad, the Tiger Triple and the Summit Triple. A new Guest Services Lodge was built adjacent to the Main Lodge; a deck and covered walkway was created as a connector between the two lodges.

The completely revamped Gunstock was unveiled to the public in 1988. The commission and the management of Gunstock had carefully planned the renovations keeping in mind that the goal was to remain competitive. What they weren't prepared for was an unanticipated series of challenging snow seasons while carrying a heavy debt load. The question of who would pay for a deficit was about to be answered. For the first time in its entire history, the recreation area was forced to ask for financial assistance from the taxpayers of Belknap County.

This move ruffled the feathers of some of those taxpayers—they were vehemently opposed to the idea of being forced to pay for the financial difficulties experienced by the facility. The Belknap Recreation Area Commission, having been renamed the Gunstock Area Commission, wasted no time finding a solution to the problem and in 1990 focused on its mission to return Gunstock to a financially independent position. Members of the commission created a Memorandum of Understanding that obligated Gunstock to a $150,000 annual payment to Belknap County plus a set percentage of revenue over $6 million.[45]

Any additions or expansions from that point forward were to be carefully considered and done only when it was fiscally responsible. It was at this point that Dick Tapply began working with the Gunstock Ski Club to help it become a completely self-sufficient ski club.

John Vorel replaced Dick Tapply as general manager in 1991. In 1998, Greg Goddard moved into the top position. He began his career at Gunstock in 1981 and was Gunstock's financial director for twelve years before becoming manager. His talented management team includes his director of operations, Doug Irving, and Bill Quigley, director of marketing and sales, who came on board in 2005.

A $4 million expansion plan was put before the Belknap County Legislative Delegation in the spring of 2003; however, residents of Belknap County hadn't forgotten Gunstock's past fiscal woes and remained hesitant about any further

Ready in 2003, Gunstock's Panorama High-Speed Detachable Quad began transporting skiers faster than ever to the summit of Gunstock Mountain. *Photo by Harrison Haas.*

expenditure of funds for expansions. The plan included the installation of the Panorama High-Speed Quad to the summit of Gunstock Mountain. The triple summit lift was to be relocated to the Pistol Complex, and night lighting was needed on two trails in that complex. The expansion was, however, approved after considerable review, and the additions were made swiftly and were finished by the start of the 2003–4 ski season.

While Gunstock was working out its financial issues, it never lost its ability to be a forerunner in innovation, for which it had received two national awards. In 2001, the facility won the National Ski Area's Sales and Marketing Award for its new learn-to-ski-and-ride program named Mountain Magic. A few years earlier in 1997, it had been garnished with a national award for the unique Noon Groom, which sent snow farmers out in their groomers for a midday groom of certain trails. On-demand grooming always takes place when trail conditions are in need of attention.

The groomed artificial snow is carefully watched and regulated in a state-of-the-art snowmaking plant that utilizes the millions of gallons of water held

With grooming no longer done by hand, snow grooming personnel consistently provide the very best conditions for skiers. *Courtesy of Gunstock Area Commission.*

Gunstock's complex snowmaking plant is built to get the snow made and the trails fully covered as quickly as possible. *Courtesy of Gunstock Area Commission.*

in reserve. It is further managed on the trails by a dedicated snowmaking team that works outside, day or night, in frigid and unforgiving conditions. Improvements to the snowmaking system continue, and each improvement ensures that the system will produce more snow while using far less resources and manpower.

In December 2009, a ribbon-cutting ceremony was held to dedicate the new Penny Pitou Silver Medal Quad, coinciding with the fiftieth anniversary of her winning two Olympic medals. Known locally as Penny's Chair, it is the second of its kind in the country and received praise from both ski instructors and students alike. Installed to service the beginner's trails, its child-friendly design and large, slow-moving chairs encourage entire families to ski together.

Two new separate organizations have put their members on the trails, adding to the diversity of the ski area. The Gunstock Freestyle Academy offers professional coaches to teach individuals all levels of skills in freestyle skiing and snowboarding. Another successful organization, the Gunstock Adaptive Skiing Program, is an all-volunteer organization dedicated to teaching the sport of skiing to individuals with physical, cognitive and emotional challenges.

The Penny Pitou Silver Medal Quad stands as a symbol of Gunstock's family-oriented mission. *Photo by Harrison Haas.*

The recreation spot returned to and remains a financially independent entity. Today, it is known as Gunstock Mountain Resort and is in the process of reinventing itself as a formidable family entertainment center offering new and exciting activities throughout the entire year. Brand new for the 2011 season was the arrival of the Gunstock Mountain Adventure Park, which includes Aerial Treetop Adventures, a complex obstacle course, games and zip lines suspended from trees. New activities include guided Segway tours and the exciting ZipTour, consisting of the longest zip lines in the continental United States.

Gunstock's survival has been based on its great ability to adapt. Greg Goddard summarized Gunstock's evolution best when he explained, "When I reflect on all of this change, I realize that this is what Gunstock has always been about, starting when our Belknap County fathers had the courage and innovation to build a major ski resort complex on Gilford farmland to stimulate the local economy and attract visitors from Boston and beyond." He couldn't have been more correct when he added, "The more things change, the more they stay the same."[46]

GUNSTOCK'S RICH SKI HISTORY

Its Preservation Is Its Future

The existence of the original construction documents of Gunstock's beginnings is remarkable. These documents will be preserved as a record of the early development of the ski industry in New Hampshire.
–Robert Durfee, Gunstock Area commissioner and professional structural engineer

My personal discovery of Gunstock's ski history began with a restoration project that our daughter, Sarah, spearheaded in 2006. She was a mere ten years old at the time. The project launched my five-year journey into this history, and I can now say that the documentation of Gunstock's evolution has become one of the most incredible and exciting experiences of my life.

Five years ago, it made no sense when our little girl became fascinated with a small red structure perched by the side of the road not far from Gilford's town hall. It obviously hadn't been used in years and was an eyesore, and she continually asked us why no one was taking care of it. Through my connections with the Thompson-Ames Historical Society in Gilford, I learned that the building and about eighteen acres of land had been donated to the town in 1994 by Gilford residents Gary and Lucile Allen.

It was recommended that I call Sheldon Morgan, the man in charge of the Public Works Department in Gilford. He explained that the small, run-down structure was the former warming hut used by the now-defunct

The historic Gilford Outing Club warm-up hut awaits restoration. *Photo by Harrison Haas.*

Gilford Outing Club. Hundreds of Gilford's children had learned to ski on the slopes behind the building. Gilford's Olympic medalist Penny Pitou was among them.

I began to search for information, wanting to have a complete picture of this organization and why it was so important to the people who had been a part of it. Very early in my research, I quickly discovered that there wasn't an abundance of written information describing the activities of the Gilford Outing Club. I began to interview local residents, and from their delightful stories and personal recollections, I could see that this piece of our town's history was pure magic. This unique story needed to be documented, and it deserved to be in the form of a book.

I also began to look into the development of Gunstock, often wondering why this ski area was created in Gilford. Yes, the Belknap Mountain Range certainly played a role, but there has never been a lack of mountains in New Hampshire, especially ones far loftier than Gunstock Mountain.

The same year, Gunstock was celebrating its seventieth anniversary. As part of its ongoing celebrations, an event called Remember When was planned. Diane Mitton, curator for Gilford's Thompson-Ames Historical Society, was already organizing the archives at Gunstock. Her work made it possible for hundreds of photographs to be displayed in an orderly fashion during Remember When.

Before the event, I was in contact with Bill Quigley, Gunstock's director of marketing and sales. The plan for Remember When was to invite the general public to the Main Lodge to look at the photos from the ski area's archives. The management and staff were trying to identify individuals in the photos and asked for the public's assistance. When I watched members of the public look at these photos, I realized that the same magic I saw in the Gilford Outing Club was also there at Gunstock. There was no doubt that the sport of skiing had had a profound effect on the local community, but I had yet to learn just how much.

During this well-attended event, Bill insisted that a book about Gunstock needed to be written. I quickly found the same thing with the history of Gunstock—there was no organized documentation of the pertinent information. It was amazing as well as frustrating to discover that no one had taken the time to write down what had happened at this great place, particularly during its early years.

The only reliable source of detailed information was found on microfilm. Newspapers from the 1920s onward provided me with the bulk of information I was desperately seeking. Day by day, page by page, the story of Gunstock revealed itself, and it was far beyond what I had expected.

I soon discovered that the sixty-meter jump was the first structure built at the Belknap Mountains Recreation Area. That looming structure was the reason Cherry Valley Road (Route 11A) became the main road through the town of Gilford, and it was the reason the road was continued through to the neighboring town of Alton. I learned that more world-class jumpers have taken flight from this jump than the same class of Alpine skiers has ever skied down the trails of Gunstock. That count of ski jumping stars is staggering.

There was never a question that the ski jump had major historical significance. Last used by the Gunstock Nordic Association in 2004, it, like the warming hut in another part of town, was falling into disrepair. I penned a short history and sent it to Gunstock's general manager, Greg Goddard. He presented this information to the five members of the Gunstock Area Commission and invited me to attend the August 2009 meeting of the commission.

Unknown to me at the time, Gunstock Area commissioner Bob Durfee was already hard at work on the preservation of the more than four hundred blueprints owned by Gunstock. The preservation of these drawings began decades ago with the amazing civic leader John Veazey. The entire collection had been piled into a corner of the county courthouse in Laconia, waiting to meet with an early demise via a quick trip to the dumpster. During the 1960s, John insisted that the blueprints be returned to Gunstock. Once safely back home, they sat in the attic of the Main Lodge for decades until Bob began the daunting task of flattening and categorizing them.

I attended that August meeting, along with Lisa Kling, head of the jumping program with Gunstock Nordic Association. Lisa's son, Jonathan, had been a top ski jumper, and it was her dream to see the return of high-level jumping competitions reminiscent of the meets that she had helped organize for many years.

The commissioners granted me permission to nominate the seventy-meter jump for the Seven to Save designation from the New Hampshire Preservation Alliance. Annually, the alliance honors seven historically significant New Hampshire properties with this designation, drawing attention to the property with the hopes of seeing it preserved. The historic jump was awarded the designation in October 2009. What followed was a tremendous response from the general public and renewed interest in the history of Gunstock at the local, regional and national levels. E-mails were received from across the country and as far away as California.

Clearly, the historic restoration of the seventy-meter jump was an epic one, and a separate organization was needed to pursue this goal. On December 23, 2009, the Gunstock Mountain Historic Preservation Society was formed. During its first year, the organization made tremendous strides in not only the preservation of the largest jump but in the rest of Gunstock's history as well. After many meetings and even more discussions, the decision was made to restore all four historic jumps at Gunstock, putting them back into use so that today's ski jumpers would have another place to train and compete. It was also decided that the organization's mission should include the preservation of any ski history in Belknap County.

An early discovery made by the organization was that another important history was being saved in conjunction with Gunstock's. Just after the preservation society was formed, Peter A. Hussey donated to the New England Ski Museum in Franconia two DVDs made from old films taken by his father,

A weathered seventy-meter jump in need of repair is being restored by the Gunstock Mountain Historic Preservation Society. *Photo by Harrison Haas.*

Philip W. Hussey Sr. Since Philip was head of the Hussey Manufacturing Company when the Belknap Mountains Recreation Area was constructed, he captured rare and valuable footage of the ski area during its infancy. Besides the film and some notes carefully put down on paper, the 176-year-old Hussey Seating Company had no record of its time spent in Gilford. With the preservation of Gunstock's history, part of the history of this company is finally being pieced together and preserved as well.

The preservation of the blueprints continues, as well as that of the thousands of historic photographs, slides, negatives, news clippings, programs and trail maps owned by Gunstock. Digitization of the archives has begun. In July 2010, the preservation society was awarded a $5,000 Conservation Plate Grant from the New Hampshire State Library to begin the process of professionally flattening and restoring the prints. Bob Durfee continues to work closely on this project and has a special interest in the blueprints since he created, as part of his job as a structural engineer, some of the modern drawings in Gunstock's archives. Handling a schedule that

Gunstock Area commissioner Bob Durfee stands among the historic treasures in the attic of Gunstock's Main Lodge while examining 1930s blueprints. *Photo by Harrison Haas.*

is already too full, he said it best himself when he told me, "I make the time for this because I care."

The most memorable event during the society's first year was the rededication of Gunstock's seventy-meter jump and the unveiling of a memorial plaque to honor legendary ski jumper Torger Tokle. The ceremony took place on March 9, 2011, the seventieth anniversary of his hill record on the big jump. In attendance were Torger's nephew Kenneth and his wife, Nina. During an emotional ceremony and before dozens of onlookers, Greg Goddard rededicated Gunstock's seventy-meter jump in honor of our country's adopted son.

The building that started this journey, the Gilford Outing Club hut, is currently being reconstructed. Fundraising is complete, materials have been purchased and work has begun. The talented students at the Huot Technical Center in Laconia, led by their teacher, Dave Dupuis, constructed the walls for the hut. The Gilford Rotary will lead the completion of the reconstruction during 2011.

Along the way, we've come to understand our daughter's fascination with that little red structure. Now at the age when college is looming on the horizon, she has decided to specialize in the preservation of historic structures. Through the research, meetings and discussions we've had on how to restore her favorite building, she has gained an understanding for the need in our society for individuals who have the knowledge of what is involved with the proper restoration of historic buildings.

Over the years it has taken me to write this book, I've made many friends with whom I share a common bond: the love of this history. Each and every one of their stories has given me incredible inspiration even in my daily life. Fortunately, there are many residents who felt that our ski history is important enough to preserve and took it upon themselves to do so in their own way.

One such person is Bob Bolduc, a lifelong resident of the Lakes Region. A well-known businessman, he—and now two of his sons—are owners of

A pulley from the Gilford Outing Club rope tow serves as a reminder of ski seasons gone by. *Photo by Harrison Haas.*

Bob Bolduc sits surrounded by many of his ski artifacts, including a small-scale model of Gilford's Cotton Hill ski jump. *Photo by Harrison Haas.*

Piche's Ski & Sport Shops. Since the first time I met him, Bob has encouraged me to keep going with my preservation efforts, continually telling me how important the local ski history is to our area. Growing up in the middle of this history, he fully understands its significance and is happiest when he's surrounded by it. His personal connection to the individuals, places and events of this history is astounding. Fittingly, a wonderful honor was awarded to him when he was inducted into the New England Ski Hall of Fame in February 2011.

I have also been fortunate to have had the opportunity to sit and have conversations with such inspiring ski icons as Penny Pitou, Gary Allen and Bernie Dion Sr., as well as Earl Norem and Bill Duncan, both brave members of the Tenth Mountain Division. With their stories, they breathed life into the information I had gathered, and I remain in awe of them. They, along with the thousands of people who are part of Gunstock's history, helped me write this book—it is the story of their lives and the choices they made along the way.

Sadly, many of our local ski greats died over the course of time it took me to complete the manuscript for this book. Gary Allen, Bill Trudgeon and Gilford Outing Club leaders Seth Keller and Wayne Snow all passed away. John Veazey, who had become such a good friend to me, died after a brief illness in December 2010. I keenly felt the loss of him as a friend, but I also felt the loss of his firsthand knowledge of the history he continually shared with me.

Losing these people made me realize that it is vital for every community to act as steward of its history; it is the responsibility of the individuals within a community to make sure that a continual effort is made. A little piece of each of us disappears when a part of our history is lost. That loss also takes away something of value from future generations who don't yet have a say in its preservation.

If there is one thing to be said of Gunstock since its inception, it is that it has transformed thousands of lives for the better, including my own. In a symbolic way, I began to understand this transformation the day the gifted writer and photographer Harrison Haas and I walked the grounds of Gunstock as he

Past meets present: modern snow guns fill the landscape with snow while overshadowing Gunstock's historic Main Lodge. *Photo by Harrison Haas.*

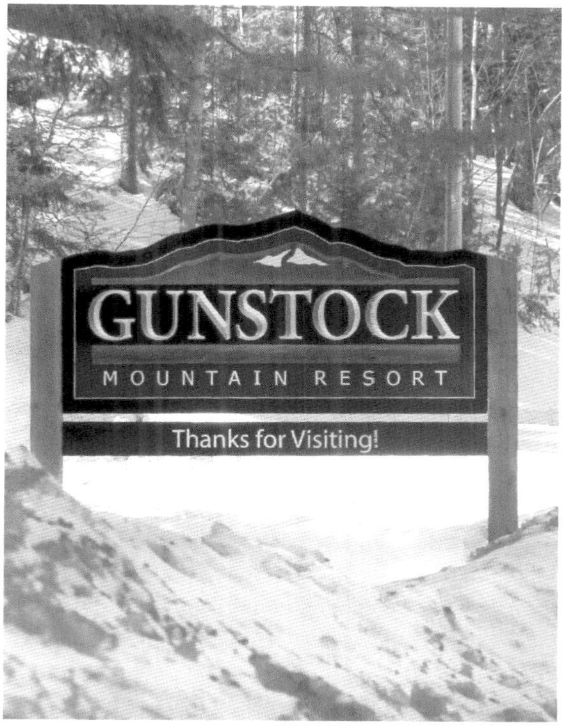

Photo by Harrison Haas.

took the contemporary images for this book. It was a cold, overcast November day, with a barren landscape still awaiting the first snowfall of the season. On that day, snowmaking had just begun at the base of the mountain. With snow guns blasting and sounding more like jet engines, we walked into a blizzard of snow. Instantly and completely the entire world became a far different place, not unlike it undoubtedly had been for all the people whose lives were forever changed by being woven into a piece of Gunstock's past.

Nothing is quite as satisfying as the preservation of any history, since it validates the thoughts, hopes, dreams and hard work of the individuals who helped shape it. As each step is taken to save the ski history of the Lakes Region, there is a certain amount of pride to be had in knowing that we wouldn't have disappointed those previous generations who tirelessly created something of value for their children and grandchildren. Having the knowledge that this history is properly preserved, we can believe in the words from one of the favorite sayings of the great Gary Allen: "The best is yet to come."

NOTES

SKIING TAKES THE LAKES REGION BY STORM

1. *Laconia Democrat*, "Ski Club Trails Win Much Praise," December 23, 1932.
2. *Laconia Evening Citizen*, "Ski Trail General Committee to Meet Tonight at Seven," December 6, 1934.

EARLY YEARS

3. Marge Muehlke, "Skiing on the West Side," *Gilford Steamer*, February 5, 2005.
4. Ebba M. Janson, "Area T-Bar Ordered 19 Years After Cooke Ran Second U.S. Tow," *Laconia Evening Citizen*, February 27, 1954.
5. *Laconia Evening Citizen*, "Gilford Ski Jump to Employ 80 Men," March 19, 1935. The Federal Emergency Relief Administration, also known as FERA, preceded the more well-known Works Progress Administration. Both federal programs offered funds to help communities put the unemployed back to work during the Great Depression.

The Creation of the Belknap Mountains Recreation Area

6. *Laconia Evening Citizen*, "Legislators Brave Heights of New Gilford Ski Jump," May 3, 1935.
7. Old Home Day is an annual gathering and parade held during the summer in most New Hampshire towns.
8. The Tourade was the combination of a parade/tour of individuals interested in learning more about the WPA project underway in the Lakes Region. It began in Laconia and ended at the recreation area, where the group participated in a tour of the entire facility.
9. *Laconia Evening Citizen*, "Main Features in Belknap Area," February 14, 1937.
10. *Laconia Evening Citizen*, "Ruud Leaves for Sun Valley, Sverre Kolterud for Banff," March 1, 1937.

The Hussey Manufacturing Company's Gift to the Lakes Region

11. Hussey, *A Long Furrow Plowed*, 71.

Transformation

12. It is a widely accepted theory that the Baraks was built for the sole purpose of housing WPA workers. To date, no documentation has been found to support this theory.
13. Nachbaur in Benton, "Development of Skiing in Gilford," 13.

Torger Tokle

14. *Time*, "Sport: Yumper," www.time.com/time/magazine/article/0,9171,789987,00.html.
15. *Laconia Evening Citizen*, "Like Coming Home to be Back in Laconia Say Ski Stars," March 7, 1942.

16. *Laconia Evening Citizen*, "Here to Report Four-Event Meet," March 7, 1942.

17. Frank Elkins, "Practise [*sic*] Six Years Before Trying to Jump From Big Hill Says Tokle," *Laconia Evening Citizen*, March 7, 1942.

18. Fred Green, "Torger Tokle Works on Docks," *Laconia Evening Citizen*, December 24, 1941.

19. *Laconia Evening Citizen*, "Taps at Meet for Torger," March 8, 1946.

20. Frank Elkins, "Torger Tokle—Our Dear Friend," *Laconia Evening Citizen*, March 8, 1946.

21. Ibid.

22. *Laconia Evening Citizen*, "Sports Award for Torger Tokle," September 25, 1945.

Growing Pains

23. *Laconia Evening Citizen*, "Chamber Opposes Sale or Lease of Recreation Area," September 29, 1943.

24. Ebba M. Janson, "County Solons to Organize Soon," *Laconia Evening Citizen*, January 10, 1945.

25. *Laconia Evening Citizen*, "Delegation Will Act on Area Bill," February 28, 1945.

26. Montana, *Archie*, 104–12.

27. The out-run is the flat area beyond the landing hill of a jump that serves as an area for ski jumpers to slow down and stop.

Fritzie Baer

28. Bob Arnold, e-mail message to author, May 2011.

29. *Laconia Evening Citizen*, "Authorize T-Bar Lift at Area," February 24, 1954.

30. *Laconia Evening Citizen*, "$5,000 Program for Improvement of Belknap Area Ski Jumps Sought," March 27, 1956.

31. Belknap County Annual Report, 1958, 70.

32. Raymond Smith, "At Hearing on County Budget Rogers Proposes Belknap Area Transfer to State or Sale," *Laconia Evening Citizen*, March 5, 1958.

33. *Laconia Evening Citizen*, "Fritzie Honored at Weirs Beach," July 6, 1959.

FIRST CHAIRLIFT IN THE EAST

34. *Laconia Evening Citizen*, "Chair Tow Latest Addition to Recreation Area Facilities," February 5, 1938.
35. *Laconia Evening Citizen*, "Expect Ski Tow Completion Jan. 15," December 1, 1937.
36. *Laconia Evening Citizen*, "Chair Tramway to be Rebuilt at Estimated Cost of $25,000," February 2, 1950.

THE GILFORD OUTING CLUB

37. Douglas P. Hill, letter to John Foley, Collection of Don Chesebrough, October 2, 1993.

PENNY PITOU

38. *Laconia Evening Citizen*, "Penny Competes in France," February 11, 1956.
39. *Laconia Evening Citizen*, "Penny Pitou, Bound for Middle East, Writes of Ski Racing in Europe," April 10, 1958.
40. *Laconia Evening Citizen*, "Penny and Betsy Ski Sensations in Switzerland," January 10, 1959.
41. *Laconia Evening Citizen*, "Wire from Pres. Eisenhower Greets Penny at State House Where She Talks to Legislature," February 26, 1959.

GUNSTOCK NORDIC ASSOCIATION AND GUNSTOCK SKI CLUB

42. Allen in Benton, "Development of Skiing in Gilford," 32.
43. FIS is the abbreviation in all languages for the International Ski Federation. The organization was founded in 1924 and monitors the growth of competitive skiing throughout the world.
44. Ruth McLaughlin, e-mail message to author, July 2011.

THE CONTINUING EVOLUTION

45. This information used to be a part of a section on the official Gunstock website called "The History of Gunstock." However, that section seems to have been taken down at the time of publication. There is still some history discussed in the FAQ at http://gunstock.com/about_us/faq.
46. Greg Goddard, e-mail message to author, July 2011.

BIBLIOGRAPHY

Allen, E. John B. *From Skisport to Skiing: One Hundred Years of an American Sport, 1840–1940*. Amherst: University of Massachusetts Press, 1993.

———. *New England Skiing*. Dover, NH: Arcadia Publishing, 1997.

———. *New Hampshire on Skis*. Portsmouth, NH: Arcadia Publishing, 2002.

Benton, Corning. "The Development of Skiing in Gilford, New Hampshire." Unpublished paper, 1994.

Hengen, Elizabeth Durfee, and Sarah Dangelas Hofe. Gunstock Mountain Resort Historic Resources Study. Unpublished, March 2011.

Howe, Nicholas. "Penny Peerless." *Skiing Heritage* 18, no. 3 (September 2006): 15–20.

Hussey, Philip W., Sr., and Philip W. Hussey Jr. *A Long Furrow Plowed: 1835–1995*. North Berwick, ME: self-published, 1995.

Hussey, Philip W. Sr., Philip W. Hussey Jr. and Timothy B. Hussey. *A Long Furrow Plowed: A History of the Hussey Seating Company, 1835–2010*. North Berwick, ME: self-published, 2010.

Montana, Bob. *Archie: The Complete Daily Newspaper Comics 1946–1948.* San Diego, CA: IDW Publishing, 2010.

Mulligan, Adair D. *The Gunstock Parish: A History of Gilford, New Hampshire.* West Kennebunk, ME: Phoenix Publishing, 1995.

Owen, A.Y. "Six on Skis, Best in U.S." *Life*, February 1960, 157–60.

Pitou, Penny. "Biographical Sketch of Penny Pitou." Unpublished paper, revised April 19, 2010.

ADDITIONAL RESOURCES

Annual Reports of Belknap County, 1945–61, from the collection of Bob Arnold.

Articles from the *Laconia Democrat* and the *Laconia Evening Citizen*, 1928–59.

Gilford Outing Club records, from the Thompson-Ames Historical Society.

Gunstock Mountain Resort. Photographs, blueprints, programs, brochure and scrapbook collections.

"Gunstock Ski Club." Unpublished paper, circa 1980.

Winnipesaukee Ski Club scrapbooks, 1936, from the Laconia Historical and Museum Society.

Interviews

Allen, Gary. Interview with author, March 2007.

Duncan, Bill. Interview with author, June 2011.

Norem, Earl. Interview with author, June 2011.

Pitou, Penny. Interview with author, September 2010.

INDEX

Z

ABOUT THE AUTHOR

Carol Lee Anderson's interest in the history of her community began when she became involved with Gilford's Thompson-Ames Historical Society, serving as a board member and vice-president. Through her research of the town's history, she realized the significance of Gilford's ski history, leading her to become a founder and first president of the Gunstock Mountain Historic Preservation Society.

Just minutes away from Gunstock, she resides in Gilford with her family and writes monthly historical articles for the *Gilford Steamer* and the *Citizen of Laconia*. She can be contacted at: www.carol@berrypatchhollow.com.